Daily Fragrance of the Lotus Flower

Daily Fragrance of the Lotus Flower

Ji Kwang Dae Poep Sa Nim

Volume 2
1993

Bo Duk Religious Research Center
Mountain View, Hawaiʻi

Energy Spiritual Writing Paintings by Ji Kwang Dae Poep Sa Nim.

Front cover: Title: *"Helping You to Become a Leader or Important Person."* Description: While Queen Maya was pregnant, one night in her dreams a six-tusked elephant appeared. Upon its back the elephant carried a most august, revered, and beautiful bodhisattva that had come from the sky. The elephant brought the bodhisattva to their royal garden. After the dream, Maya knew she would give birth to an important son. *Acrylic on canvas.*

Back cover: Title: *"Good Luck."* Description: Spiritually, this is a very powerful painting. For good luck and prosperity and that 10,000 things may turn out well. *Acrylic on canvas.*

First Published in 2012
by Bo Duk Religious Research Center
P. O. Box 787
Mountain View, HI 96771 USA

© 2012 Ji Kwang Dae Poep Sa Nim
ISBN: 978-1-936843-03-9
ISSN: 2159-0869

All rights reserved. No part of this book may be reproduced or transmitted in any form or by any means, electronic or mechanical, including photocopying and recording, or in any information storage or retrieval system, without prior written permission from the publishers.

Author's Opening

Dear Reader,
In the clear, crisp night sky each individual star shines brightly, adorning the heavens with its beauty. The radiance of each star encompasses the whole world and brings forth a beautiful mind for anyone whose gaze takes in the brilliance of the stars, making that person and everyone else happy.

It is just like this: each person is also like one of the bright, shining stars in the beautiful night sky. Without any stars, there is little beauty in the night sky, and the sky itself loses much of its value.

Each individual person is as important as each shining star that gives beauty to all sentient beings. Each person that eliminates his or her impurities by practicing sincerely will become clearer and brighter and ever more radiant. Each practicing person will become like a bright, shining star in the dark sky.

Since July 17, 1992, without missing a single day, through Buddha's message I have been writing the Daily Sutras to help bring out the wisdom that is within each and every one of us.

Each teaching is like a simple reminder that helps you throughout the daily ups and downs of your busy lives, so that in the end you can become like a bright, shining star.

All of the teachings fit the energy of the particular day they are written. Yet, as you read the teachings gathered here, you will see that each and every one of them is actually timeless. These always timely teachings help you by offering beautifully simple ways of understanding and grasping the perplexity of our daily lives as we deal with others, in friendships, in love relationships, in our work, and in pursuing self realization.

As you read these teachings you will see that they are not only for students of Buddhism. They can be applied by anyone, regardless of background, religion, age or gender.

I hope that you enjoy reading these teachings and become your own bright shining star.

Ji Kwang Dae Peop Sa Nim

Foreword

The Daily Fragrance of the Lotus Flower is a comprehensive collection of the daily teachings that have been offered by Ji Kwang Dae Poep Sa Nim, the Supreme Matriarch of the Yun Hwa Denomination of World Social Buddhism, since July 17, 1992. Divided into yearly volumes, this collection is a treasure-store of daily life wisdom. Each teaching is, in truth, a "daily sutra" authored by Ji Kwang Dae Poep Sa Nim in enlightening response to the life issues and questions of Her students and to the shifting complexion of local, national and world events. Whereas the teachings of the historical Buddha — Siddhārtha Gautama or Shakyamuni Buddha — were memorized by His students and passed down orally for generations before being committed to writing, the daily teachings of Ji Kwang Dae Poep Sa Nim have been written by Her own hand, each and every morning, in immediate response to the energy and issues of the day.

This is the second of a precious series of yearly volumes of *The Daily Fragrance of the Lotus Flower* that will be published in an ongoing fashion. Each of the teachings in each volume expresses both the means-to and the meaning-of unblemished clarity and unhindered compassion. As daily sutras, these teachings at once demonstrate enlightened engagement with the relational dynamics of daily life and offer directly useful methods for realizing that there are ultimately no impediments to transforming every situation into the bodhimandala, or "place of enlightenment." Respectfully received and mindfully read, the teachings collected in these volumes are an illumination from within of our ever-changing human situation — a revelation of the suchness (*tathātā*) of daily life and the incomparable and unending path of appreciative and contributory virtuosity.

Social Buddhism

Social Buddhism is the Dharma (Teaching) of daily life wisdom. Social Buddhism is not above sentient beings, and it is not below sentient beings; it is within and together with sentient beings in order to eliminate ignorance and to attain and skillfully enact wisdom.

The origin of Social Buddhism dates back to the time of Shakyamuni Buddha. The Buddha's recorded teachings (Pali: *suttas*; Sanskrit: *sutras*) reveal the Buddha interacting with and providing wise and compassionate guidance to people from all levels of society — from manual laborers to royalty — in meadows, on mountain peaks, in parks, private homes and palaces. All of these teachings take the form of conversations between the Buddha, his disciples, both ordained and lay students, and people living in the villages, towns and cities that he visited. Most often, the teachings begin with the Buddha being asked a question emerging from the daily life experiences of those fortunate enough to meet him. Thus, from its very beginnings, Buddhism has been socially engaged. Today, Social Buddhism is most thoroughly exemplified by the teachings and practices of the Supreme Matriarch Ji Kwang Dae Poep Sa Nim of the Yun Hwa Denomination of World Social Buddhism. This volume and those to follow collect the Daily Sutras offered by Ji Kwang Dae Poep Sa Nim to Her students and to the rest of the world. They are a treasure house of contemporary daily life wisdom.

Social Buddhism is Omniscient Buddhism and the most encompassing form of Buddhism, embracing teachings and practices from Theravada, Mahayana, Vajrayana and Zen Buddhist traditions. As in other forms of Buddhism, Social Buddhism joins monks and nuns and laypersons through the teachings of Buddha (which means 'the absolute,' 'the truth'), the study of *suttas* or *sutras*, meditation practice, and (as in Zen) the formal teaching of koans (Korean: *kongan*; Chinese: *gongan*). In Social Buddhism, one has to know and honor both the Dharma taught by the Buddha, and the ethical precepts (Vinaya) that inform the Buddhist community (Sangha). But one must also know and honor the customs and manners appropriate in each place and at each time. First and foremost, however, Social Buddhism teaches the means-to and the meaning-of living a correct life every single day, exemplifying a correct mind moment-by-moment.

What distinguishes Social Buddhism from other forms of Buddhism is that the Social Buddhist doctrine is so direct, pure and true (encompassing) that it is able to improvise fluently with the patterns and dynamics of contemporary life, while resolutely guiding people onto the path of Buddha. Unlike traditions that have come to be tightly bound up with specific cultural norms and constrained by fixed paradigms and dogmas rigidly adhered to for centuries, Social Buddhism is flexible enough to respond to people's minds as they have come to be through each person's individual karma, all while following the original Dharma of Shakyamuni Buddha.

In order to have a correct life, one must follow three kinds of practice.

1. Keeping the precepts.
2. Having a meditation mind and dwelling in quietude.
3. Attaining wisdom in order to eliminate ignorance.

If one does not keep the precepts, one's mind becomes hindered and bothered, making it difficult for one to be clear. When one's mind is not in quietude, it is constantly undulating, also rendering one unclear. Finally, dissolving ignorance — the root of trouble and suffering — requires wisdom. That is why these three categories of practice are so important. They are the foundation of Social Buddhism.

While Shakyamuni Buddha was alive, Buddhism most commonly took the form of an ascetic practice reserved for monks and nuns. During the first three-month retreat after Shakyamuni Buddha's *parinirvana* (ultimate release), his students held a Council to recite collectively all the teachings of the Buddha remembered by those present. Roughly 100 years later, a second Council was held to establish a comprehensive canon of the Buddha's teachings. About a half-century later (in the middle of the third century BCE), as a result of disputes about the Vinaya, or rules for monks and nuns, different denominations of Buddhism began to appear.

Mahayana Buddhism began to emerge as a distinct set of teachings and practices about 100 years later in the second century BCE. Over this same period of time, what is now known as Theravada also became established as a distinct tradition. As in the Buddha's original Sangha, Mahayana Buddhism was taught to everyone, regardless of their social status, but still followed the strict ascetic practices associated with Theravada Buddhism. Also, whereas the

Theravada accorded great respect to the *arahants,* or students of the Buddha who realized the meaning of Buddhist practice and liberation, the Mahayana offered greatest reverence to *bodhisattvas,* or beings who dedicate themselves to skillfully-assisting all sentient beings in the realization of liberation.

Although the peoples of Korea may have long had contact with Buddhism through the Silk Roads trade that linked India, Central Asia and East Asia, Mahayana Buddhism was formally introduced to Korea from China by an imperial mission sent during the Korean Goguryeo Dynasty in 372. Buddhism was quickly embraced in Goguryeo and the other kingdoms that existed during the same period on the Korean peninsula, Baekje and Silla. During the Three Kingdoms period, in addition to the Chinese imperial mission that sent Buddhist texts and images to Korea, Korean masters were also traveling to China, bringing back Buddhist teachings.

Buddhism was first formally adopted as a state religion in 529, when the king of Silla officially embraced Buddhism. A court noble named Ichadon was to be executed because of his Buddhist faith. He informed his executioner that to believe in Buddha is the truth, and that as proof of this, white blood would spill from his body once they carried out his execution. White blood did flow from Ichadon's body, and King Beopheung (514–540) was so impressed that he decided to make Buddhism the official state religion of Silla in 529.

From Korea, Buddhism spread to other parts of East Asia, and by the 7th century was well established throughout the region. During the Unified Silla Dynasty, two great masters Uisang (625–702) and Wonhyo (617–686) traveled to Tang Dynasty China and officially brought key Buddhist teachings back to Korea, including the Flower Ornament or Avatamsaka Sutra. Uisang founded the Wonyung (Hwa-eom; Chinese, Huayan) School that has been the foundation for Korean Buddhist doctrinal traditions to the present day. Wonhyo sought to synthesize various Buddhist teachings in an all-inclusive vision and to combine these with Buddhist practices that were effective in daily life as well as in monastic settings.

Bodhidharma, who was the twenty-eighth patriarch in India, exemplified the third form of Buddhism which came to be known as Chan (in China), Zen (in Japan) or Seon (in Korea). Bodhidharma lived during the fifth century. From South India, Bodhidharma traveled to China to see King Wu of the Liang Dynasty (Yan Mun Che) and began to teach Buddhism there, becoming known thereafter as the first patriarch of Chan Buddhism. Before Bodhidharma's arrival, the Chinese studied and practiced various traditions of Mahayana Buddhism, and especially emphasized carrying out bodhisattva actions and building up virtue. King Yan Mu Che was very happy that a great master like Bodhidharma would arrive from India. The king told Bodhidharma that he built many temples, funded Buddhist translation work and did many bodhisattva actions. The king wanted to know how much virtue he had created through all these actions. Bodhidharma told him that he made "no virtue." The king was infuriated and told Bodhidharma, "You said that my virtue is nothing, but you are supposed to be a great master and the twenty-eighth Patriarch. In fact, who are you?" Bodhidharma told the king, "I am nothing." The king did not understand this profound response and the true teaching Bodhidharma was offering to him. Instead, the king only had murderous thoughts, and Bodhidharma left the southeastern coast of China and traveled north to Mount Song (or Sorim Mountain) near the Chinese capital of Luoyang. There he meditated for nine years without once touching the wall with his back to show the value of the practice and the meaning of Zen. Bodhidharma's teaching centered on realizing the one true nature of all things, understanding karma and practicing mindfulness in all situations.

Bodhidharma did not seek students, but one young man named Hea Ga (Huiko) is said to have cut off his arm in the snow to show how much he wanted to learn from Bodhidharma. Bodhidharma decided to teach him, and Hae Ga went on to become recognized as the second patriarch of Zen Buddhism in China. Bodhidharma's lineage became prominent in China with the sixth patriarch, Huineng, who focused on realizing one's own true nature and demonstrating sudden enlightenment or readiness for awakening (*dunwu*). The Chan tradition developed many branches, but enlightened masters like Baizhang, Huangbo, Mazu and Linji came to figure in all the lineages transmitted into Korea and Japan. Chan (Japanese: Zen; Korean: Seon) Buddhism centers on meditation and a special mind-to-mind transmission, beyond words and letters; but Chan also respected the history of Buddhism, attainment of the truth of the sutras and the importance of an enlightened teacher in realizing one's true self. According to Chan, if one does not have clear teaching and guidance, one can easily fall into debilitating vacuity.

Buddhism in Korea went through its most difficult time during the Yi Dynasty (Joseon) (1392–1910), because the dynasty's founder,

King Yi Seong Gye (1335–1408), adopted Confucianism and demoted Buddhism from its position as the national religion. During the earlier Goryeo Dynasty (918–1392), temples were located in villages and were a central part of everyday life. It was not until the Yi Dynasty that temples were forced to move into the mountains. Confucianism existed during the Goryeo Dynasty, but it was not officially recognized as a state religion as in the Joseon.

A key moment for Social Buddhism occurred when the great master Dae Gak Guksa (Uicheon), who was the fourth son of Goryeo Emperor Munjong, traveled to China during the Song Dynasty (1086). Dae Gak Guksa returned from China as a strong advocate of the Cheontae (Chinese: Tiantai; Japanese: Tendai) School, which had adopted the Lotus Sutra as its central scripture. On his return, he established the Cheontae Denomination as a distinct tradition. Cheontae, which quickly became a major, syncretic force in Korean Buddhism, combined an emphasis on meditation (central to Seon/Chan/Zen) and non-duality (central to Hwa-eom/Huayan). It later branched out into several other denominations. Among these new branches was the Poep Hwa Denomination.

Supreme Matriarch Ji Kwang Dae Poep Sa Nim was a student of the Poep Hwa Denomination and eventually received the title of archbishop. Soon thereafter, the Supreme Patriarch of the Poep Hwa Denomination handed down the lineage and Patriarch Kim Gap Yol gave Ji Kwang Dae Poep Sa Nim the title of Supreme Matriarch.

When Supreme Matriarch Ji Kwang Dae Poep Sa Nim came to the West (first to the United States of America and then to Europe), She brought not only the lineage of Cheontae Poep Hwa:

through Her attainment, She realized that global conditions were opportune for revitalizing Shakyamuni Buddha's method of daily teaching in the context of everyday life and for a new flowering of His unbroken lineage of Social Buddhism. To symbolize this, Supreme Matriarch Ji Kwang Dae Poep Sa Nim decided to change the name of Her Cheontae Poep Hwa denomination to Yun Hwa or Lotus Flower. While Poep Hwa means Dharma Flower, the original symbol of Buddhism is the blossoming of the lotus. Supreme Matriarch Ji Kwang Dae Poep Sa Nim is the first Matriarch of the Yun Hwa Denomination of World Social Buddhism.

Social Buddhism has existed since the time of Shakyamuni Buddha. Although Shakyamuni Buddha wanted to teach Social Buddhism, he had to respond to the people living during that period and the quality of their thoughts and mindfulness. Because of their ideologies and concepts, Shakyamuni Buddha had to stress a stricter and more ascetic teaching and practice. Similarly, when Dae Poep Sa Nim first began accepting students in Honolulu, they just wanted good luck and ceremonies, but were not really interested in learning the Dharma. It was not until later, in 1984, when Dae Poep Sa Nim traveled to Europe, that She found students who were open to learning the true Dharma.

During the time of Shakyamuni Buddha, one of His lay students, Vimalakirti, taught a form of Social Buddhism, and Shakyamuni Buddha was very appreciative of that. Shakyamuni Buddha even sent Moon Soo Bodhisattva (Manjusri), the bodhisattva of awareness and wisdom, to attend Vimalakirti. But even Vimalakirti was not able to develop Social Buddhism to its full extent because the mind of the people was inclined more toward ascetic practice.

Social Buddhism is unique in providing the daily life wisdom to perform one's correct function and duties as a human being while also attaining enlightenment. Without going into the mountains and living apart from society, one can live one's daily life and yet also be able to see oneself and reflect upon oneself correctly. One can realize the highest levels of attainment in the very midst of the social world through cultivating true and clear relationships. Social Buddhism is truly boundless.

Supreme Matriarch Ji Kwang Dae Poep Sa Nim is recognized by many to be one of the few masters since Shakyamuni Buddha who has dared to teach and demonstrate what Social Buddhism is by being a living exemplar.

For example, until now, masters and particularly patriarchs or matriarchs always have had to wear formal Dharma robes as part of the Buddhist tradition. The traditional clothing worn by matriarchs and patriarchs is used to show their status and to insure that they receive the proper respect for their attainment. But when Supreme Matriarch Ji Kwang Dae Poep Sa Nim came to Europe, She wore the traditional clothing of a master when She was teaching, but also went beyond the tradition and wore layperson's clothes. Bringing to life the teaching of Chan Master Linji that Buddhist realization means being a "true person of no-rank," Supreme Matriarch Ji Kwang Dae Poep Sa Nim thus demonstrated the bodhisattva meaning of according with every situation and responding as needed. Moment by moment, simply and directly, Her teaching is tirelessly translating the true meaning of Social Buddhism into virtuosic action.

Because of Her great enlightenment, Supreme Matriarch Ji Kwang Dae Poep Sa Nim makes no disparaging differentiations or discriminations among religions or beliefs; everybody and everything is the same, and is part of one world and one universe. This is a truth that has been proclaimed throughout humanity. Social Buddhism teaches that activating the truth of non-duality is realizing that all beings are the same, precisely because they can differ-from and differ-for one another. Through mutual contribution and appreciation, this very situation can become a living paradise.

Secretary Monks
Lotus Buddhist Monastery

Daily Fragrance of the Lotus Flower

Volume 2
1993

"What I am teaching you is not new. You heard about it before in either this or a past life. This daily teaching is simply to remind us so that we can be clear and live correctly in this and future lives. Believing this teaching is entirely the decision of the one who reads it. In addition, applying one's own concept to this teaching is the choice of the reader himself or herself."

— *Ji Kwang Dae Poep Sa Nim*

224. January 1, 1993. Honolulu

Happy New Year!

Everyone: become a Buddha yourself, find true happiness, and adorn this present world with true beauty.

This new year, strive to use your time and space for others. When, in the midst of busy social life, you strive to use your time and space for others, your time and space are:

1. the path of eliminating one's delusion;
2. the path of fulfilling the duty of one's present form;
3. the path of realizing why you are born in this world;
4. the path of eliminating I, my, me;
5. the path of finding no I, my, me;
6. the path of finding our true place, which is our true I;
7. the path of finding the (.) in the true I.

225. January 2, 1993. Honolulu

Once upon a time there was a very arrogant man named Son O Kong. He was always jealous of the Buddha's wisdom and tried to surpass him. He used all kinds of methods and went all over the place looking for the way to satisfy his desire.

One day he finally climbed to the top of a high mountain. He told himself, "I am now on this high mountain; I am higher and wider than the Buddha." He felt really good and thought that he had finally surpassed the Buddha.

At that time the Buddha was having a siesta. Suddenly his right thumb itched. When he opened his eyes he saw Son O Kong on his thumb, holding onto and scratching it. The Buddha said, "Ay, ay, ay!

That is very dangerous; you might fall. Come down from there and RELAX, RELAX."

Suddenly Son O Kong realized that he had been doing nothing but going around the Buddha's palm. He was deeply embarrassed and realized his mistake of being arrogant and trying to surpass the Buddha.

So this New Year put down your arrogance, anger and jealousy. Get out from your own karma wall and become a big Buddha. And when you meet someone like Son O Kong, have pity for him, and give him great love and help.

Arrogance, anger and jealousy make one small. When you put them down you become a big Buddha.

226. January 3, 1993. Honolulu

Those who are successful and happy in relationships in this world are people who:
1. have someone to love;
2. have someone who loves them;
3. have someone to understand;
4. have someone who understands them;
5. have someone who is able to help them;
6. receive help from someone but have no feelings of obligation towards that person;
7. have someone with whom they can stay 24 hours a day and be comfortable without burden or bother.

Whoever has the above seven things is someone who is successful in relationships.

If you have no thinking about your own existence or that of others, and yet you are still able to concentrate and do your daily duties one hundred percent, and are also always able to deal with others with a smile, then you are the most successful person in this world.

227. January 4, 1993. Honolulu

Those who have many conditions and a wanting mind always want to show off. But others always find out what such people are really after; when this becomes obvious, it makes those with a wanting mind look bad.

Even though someone who has no conditions and who does not want many things does not try to show off, he or she nevertheless will be recognized and respected by others. Someone like this will accomplish whatever he or she wants.

If you have many conditions and a wanting mind, go for the O. When you attain that, you will get everything you want, you will be respected by others, and you will be a hero for them. You will shine everywhere, even though you do not want to show off.

228. January 5, 1993. Honolulu

We human beings come from the place of love. But when human beings do not know this, they make bad speech, action and thinking, dirtying this place of love; then they cannot live a correct life, and they suffer forever.

If you want to eliminate suffering and perform human beings' correct function, adorn this place of love with beauty. We must first realize that our original place is the place of love, and remember that we are always living there. When we realize this, our speech, action and thinking automatically become beautiful, and we become one with our original place of love. Then we can do our human beings' duty and adorn this present world with true beauty.

229. January 6, 1993. Honolulu

This I exists in empty space and goes together with time. When this I does not know how to use time and space, we waste them, dirtying them without appreciation and making this I suffer.

But if this I knows how to appreciate and use time and space, this I's suffering disappears and, in return, time and space become ever more helpful.

When you want to know the method of correctly using time and space, you must first realize that we are living in the world of opposites. So, first we have to rescue this I from the world of opposites. That is, when someone makes a mistake or when someone hurts you, do not get caught by that mistake by blaming him for it. Immediately see yourself and simply do what you have to do in that moment and the next moment.

This is rescuing yourself from the world of opposites. And at the same time, it is fixing other peoples' mistake. This is the correct method of using time and space and of living continuously and correctly in them.

230. January 7, 1993. Honolulu

Forgive those who bother practice people and make them suffer. Do not only think badly about those who bother you; find the reason they do so.

When someone bothers you in this life, it is to pay back the debt you have with him from the last life. In order to pay back your debt, do not fight with that person. First, repent for the wrong you have done to others, and practice for those who presently bother you so that they do not create more karma of bothering others.

Whoever bothers others causes himself or herself to suffer. Have pity for that ignorance; help it to disappear so that it does not perpetuate itself. Do not forget to practice for those who bother you, but practice also for those help you. When you receive help from others, to that extent you owe them.

Be a completely free person, helping others without making owing-karma for either yourself or for them.

231. January 8, 1993. Honolulu

Relax everything.
Put down everything.
Look at the sky and look at the ocean.
Look at yourself.
Come out of the spider web.
Think about it again.
Which one is the correct path?
Relax again.
Take one step now.

Put it down again.
Take another step.
Now you can see the wide path.
Comfortably take your steps.
1, 2, 3...

From now on do not relax and do not put it down. Keep going until you are satisfied.

232. January 9, 1993. Honolulu

The dharma comes from the O and makes I, which lives by depending upon the dharma.

When you know the dharma, you know I; when you do not know the dharma, you do not know I. When you eliminate the dharma, this I is eliminated. When this I is eliminated, then you know the O. So this O becomes I and this I lives eternally without the dharma, becomes a no-dharma dharma king, and creates its own dharma. When you live like this, you are a truly liberated person.

233. January 10, 1993. Honolulu.

Unclear people always want to show off and at the same time want others to understand them. And, even though an unclear person says correct things, his or her speech irritates others and drives them away.

Even though a clear person may not speak correctly, others always want to listen. A clear person's incorrect speech serves as a great teaching for others and, at the same, time gives them courage and makes them happy.

The reason for this difference is: unclear people always want to show that they are right, and this desire comes from ego. But a clear person always wants to help bring others forward and help them shine.

234. January 10, 1993. Honolulu

Do not try to find the holy person in the devil.
Find the devil in the devil.
When you find the devil and know what the devil is, you
    become *lonely-holy*.
The *lonely-holy* person again goes into the devil,
wears the devil-mask,
rescues all the devils,
and makes everyone *lonely-holy*.

235. January 11, 1993. Honolulu

While practicing, practice people have much more fear than they did before.

Fear comes from lack of clarity. When you are unclear, you make a lot of mistakes and don't realize whether you are doing wrong or right. But as you become clear through the practice, you are able to see your mistakes. Seeing your mistakes, you have fear.

When you have fear, instead of getting caught by it, strive to fix your mistakes. When you strive to do so, your past mistakes will disappear, and you will not make the same mistakes again in the future. While you are fixing your mistakes in this way, your fear will disappear and you will be able to live brightly and confidently, every day.

Practice means sorting through and taking care of everything that you have done, including your mistakes. As practice deepens, you will become free from everything.

236. January 12, 1993. Honolulu

When you make conditions, you cannot see the O.
When you eliminate conditions, you can see the O.
But when you eliminate conditions, you cannot see I.
If you can see how vast that I-which-you-cannot-see is, at that time you can make conditions. These conditions can eliminate others' conditions. Then you can put everyone into the O and make them comfortable.

When you have no-I, others want to give you I.
When you have I, others want to take it away.

237. January 13, 1993. Honolulu

Twice a day, morning and night, come out of the spider web and look at yourself:
1. See what kind of situation you are now in.
2. See what your duties and responsibilities are.
3. See if you are correctly fulfilling your duties and responsibilities.

Also, see twice a day if your situation is yin or yang. If it is yang, lower yourself. If it is yin, eliminate your I and only concentrate for and help others. Then your situation will become yang again. Once you master this method, you can live without being hindered by yin or yang.

238. January 14, 1993. Honolulu
The method for having successful human relationships

The form of each one of the trees in the forest is different.

Some are round. Some are sharp. Some are rectangular. If among those, you like only the round trees, you get caught by the sharp and rectangular ones. That is, if you do not like the sharp and rectangular trees, you cannot get the round ones.

If you want to get everything without getting caught by anyone, do not only look at the shape; just see the tree. And remember, no matter what kind of shape the trees have, you can use them in any situation and any place.

Be thankful to all of the trees.

239. January 15, 1992. Honolulu

Widely open your mind door. The wider you open your mind, the more comfortable and accommodating a person you become. When your mind door is narrowly open, your life path is rough.

When you get caught by many things, put those hindrances in the garbage can, wash your hands, and then go open your mind door as widely as possible.

Everyone goes on the same path, whether their door is widely or narrowly open. So you might as well open your door widely and proceed unhindered.

And remember, that widely open door is always round.

240. January 16, 1993. Honolulu

In that mind which is higher than the sky and deeper than the ocean, how can you try to verify what is right or wrong, true or false? When right, keep it as right; when wrong, keep it as wrong; when true, keep it as true; when false, keep it as false.

Accept whatever comes and do not stop going on your path. Proceed step by step, without getting caught. Just go.

When you become clear, even if something is wrong you can make it correct, and if something is false you can make it true.

Have fun while going on your path.

241. January 17, 1993. Honolulu

No matter how much you try to polish yourself, it is difficult to be satisfied. The more you polish, the more you see your mistakes. When you see the mistakes you made, you regret that you were so ignorant and you wish to be smarter than that.

At that time do not be regretful; do not get caught by your regret. Being regretful deepens your ignorance. Instead of being regretful, see your regret as your master. That mind which can see regret as your master will not regret anymore and will lead you onto a more profound path leading to a bright and clear future.

242. January 18, 1993. Honolulu

Wedding Poem

Correct situation	*Yin* and *yang* become one, east and west become one, man and woman become one.
	So, which one is *yin*, which one is *yang*? Which one is east, which one is west? Which one is man, which one is woman?
Correct function	Everything becomes absolutely equal. It makes the whole world comfortable, tranquil and brightly shining.
Correct relation	Now I can see your face so clearly. Oh beautiful you! How are you? May I serve you this *yin* and *yang* cake? Open your mouth.
Moment to moment	Ahhh! Mmmm! Good, good!!
Absolute energy	I love you all infinitely!

243. January 19, 1992. Honolulu

The small sailing boat, wrestling with the wind and the waves in the ocean, finally wins over them and smoothly sails into the harbor. There it relaxes for a while, forgets about the past struggle with the wind and waves and again sails out to the ocean. This is the correct function of a sailing boat.

But if this sailing boat remembers the struggle it had before and cannot sail out to the ocean again, it loses its correct function. Human life is similar to this. Forget whatever happened before, and do not be fearful of what may happen in the future. Just go on, again and again.

244. January 20, 1993. Honolulu

When you look at human beings in a good way, your mind becomes comfortable. When you look at human beings in a bad way, your mind becomes very bad. When you want to be good but your path is not deep, if others are not good, your good mind disappears and becomes bad.

If you really want to be good, look at all human beings, whether they are good or bad, in a beautiful way. When you are able to look at them this way, no matter how much others hurt and make you sad, your soreness disappears.

The mind without soreness can rescue others who are bad.

245. January 21, 1993. Honolulu

When someone hates or does not like you, do not try to win over that person. Instead, put your head down to that person. When you are able to do that, your path is getting deeper.

Through your action, the other person is able to realize his mistake and, at the same time, you also are able to realize your mistake.

Putting your head down gives others and yourself space. Putting your head down is the beauty of harmonizing good and bad actions. This action is beyond discussion.

246. January 22, 1993. Honolulu

When you look at this world, it is very bright and clean. But human beings' thinking is far from being bright and clean and is inclined to enter dark valleys. Remaining in such valleys is to live a hustling and bustling life and then disappear.

This is very sad, and it is the reason Buddha and Kwan Se Um Bo Sal are sad. Their tears of sadness become rain, and when the situation is especially depressing, they make thunder and lightning, trying to wake us up even for just a while. But human beings' thinking does not realize Buddha and Kwan Se Um Bo Sal's intention and only has the direction of going into the darkness.

So practice people, try to understand this and put your thinking into the bright and clean place. Try to get out of the dark valley as soon as possible; keep correct human thinking and make this world bright and clean.

Bright thinking eliminates one's I. That thinking makes one hundred peoples' thinking bright.

$$1 + 100 = -100$$
$$101 - 1 = +100$$

$$\diagdown \mid \diagup$$
$$\text{———}$$
$$\diagup \mid \diagdown$$

247. January 23, 1993. Honolulu

This new year, have a lot of prosperity, health and wealth, and let all of your wishes come true. Go onto the deeper path of practice, get Enlightenment, and adorn this world with beauty.

ALWAYS PUT IT DOWN.
ALWAYS RELAX.

When a hen sits on her eggs, she only concentrates on them. So this year, only concentrate on practice and practice. Then, just as when the rooster crows, darkness disappears and the bright morning comes.

As soon as possible, get out of your dark karma, see the bright world, live for others and have an appreciative life.

248. January 24, 1993. Honolulu

I feel sorry for the Buddha because I try to live wisely and in a good way, but sentient beings' social life makes me angry a lot of times, jealous and uncomfortable, and makes Buddha's bright and clear place very dirty and dizzy.

When you are angry and jealous, you do not realize you are dirtying Buddha's place. When jealousy and anger disappear, you then realize you made Buddha's place dirty; sorry and regretful, and you promise yourself never to do so again.

This promising mind eliminates your ignorance. So, when you are angry and jealous, always remember your promise that you do not want to dirty Buddha's place.

249. January 25, 1993. Las Vegas

"I love you...."

Whether true or false, do not doubt or calculate about this sentence. Just accept "I love you" as it is. Whether it is Buddha's love, sentient beings' love or animals' love, all love comes from only one place, which is the absolute world.

The person who has a lot of karma is always far away from love and does not know what true love is. This is why some people have no love for others and, at the same time, do not even have love for themselves. This is why when someone says "I love you," some people cannot accept it for what it is and always place conditions on that love. They calculate about and doubt the love, turning and going far away from it, and then they begin doubting even themselves.

So for those who do not have love and who do not know love: when someone says "I love you," just accept it as it is. Try to learn what love is and say to others, "I love you." "I love you" eliminates your karma and brings you closer to love, soon enabling you to understand what Buddha's true love is and to love others truly.

250. January 26, 1993. Las Vegas

Keep the mind that, wherever you go and whatever you do, you always do it for others and to make others happy.

This mind eliminates your karma and will carry you away from your darkness. At the same time, this action benefits you and opens the path of making yourself happy.

Life is short, death is long. In this short life, the greediness of living only for yourself shortens your life and lengthens your death.

251. January 27, 1993. Las Vegas

"Adorn with beauty this Buddha land" does not only refer to beautifying the world around us; it is meant for human beings' minds too. When human beings' minds are clean, this world becomes clean; when human beings' minds are beautiful, this world becomes beautiful.

If you really want to adorn with true beauty, build a temple in your mind and adorn your mind's Buddha land with beauty.

This is the truth of adorning this Buddha land with beauty. So practice regularly in your own mind temple, and always try to adorn it with true, bright and clear beauty.

252. January 28, 1993. Las Vegas

The supernatural power of absolute energy can create anything. Sometimes that power creates through form, and sometimes without form, through only causes and conditions and yin and yang nature's energy.

When human beings put everything down, when they do not think about themselves, when nothing hinders them and they have a completely free mind, then they can use this supernatural penetration power.

This supernatural penetration power comes only through your practice. When you are able to use this supernatural penetration power, you even forget the power that you have. With that forgetting mind, penetrating power comes automatically, and that mind will create anything, without wanting anything.

253. January 29, 1993. Las Vegas

The place human beings' thinking concentrates—put your mind into that place of concentrated thinking, follow that mind, and practice.

Then, in accord with this thinking everything will be accomplished. This thinking makes magnificent, supernatural penetration power. The master of this thinking is not your mind; it is Buddha's mind.

When you concentrate on the thinking that you have, you will forget about yourself, transcend the world of opposites and become one with the mind. This mind is not your mind; this is Buddha's mind, which is absolute world's mind. That is why Buddha and sentient beings are not two; they are one. This oneness makes true I, which is the eternal true I, which is beyond form.

254. January 30, 1992. Honolulu

Human beings have all different kinds of characteristics, but mostly you can divide them two ways. On one side are people who are much more *yin*, and on the other side are people who are much more *yang*.

People who are stronger on the *yang* side usually receive lots of respect and credit from others; they succeed more quickly, but sometimes they make a lot of mistakes. People who are stronger on the *yin* side do not get love from others very much; they succeed more slowly, but they make fewer mistakes.

Always try to perceive if you are more on the *yin* side or you are more on the *yang* side. If you are *yin*, try to change yourself to *yang*; if you are *yang*, try to get away from the *yang*. Become unhindered, without being attached to either side.

When you deal with people who have a lot of *yin*, do so in a *yin* way while helping them to get away from *yin*. When you deal with people who have a lot of *yang*, do so in a *yang* way while helping them get away from the *yang*.

Become a free person so you can use yin and yang energy as you wish, living a bright and clear life, everyday.

255. January 31, 1993. Honolulu

Just because you have so many things to do while living life, do not complain about it. Also, do not complain because you did so many things.

Whatever things come in front of you, try to do them all, one by one. The things which come in front of you do so because they are related to you. Even when you have too many things to do and it is difficult, do not be afraid; just do them.

Doing is life. Before we came into this world, we already had a lot of vacation. After death and until rebirth, we will always have a long vacation. So while you are here, whatever comes in front of you, just do it and do it.

256. February 1, 1993. Honolulu

There is an old oriental saying, "When a woman marries and goes to her in-laws' house to become a good daughter-in-law, she must not speak for three years, not hear for three years and not see for three years. Then, after nine years, she becomes a true daughter-in-law and part of the family."

This means that while you are practicing, if you want to find yourself, you need to transcend these sensations from the body—what you speak, what you hear and what you see. While you go through this, you have a lot of suffering and difficulty, but with patience you can find your true self. With this true self you become a complete, liberated human being.

P. S. This process is not only for realizing enlightenment, it is also for relationships and success in life. You need this process. With patience and practice you can accomplish anything you want. Also, the nine years are very important; that is why people say that after ten years the water and the mountain change.

257. February 2, 1993. Honolulu

Going from the world of opposites to the nirvana world is not the only path of practice.

Going from the world of opposites to the nirvana world is the path of going into the non-self world. This practice is to eliminate sufferings and attachments in the world of opposites. This path is only for self-rescue.

When you become successful in the path of self-rescue, you must completely forget the past and having been in the world of opposites.

When you attain the nirvana world, with that bright, clear mind, you must go back very deeply into the world of opposites, like the tip of a needle. When you go back into the world of opposites very deeply, you can truly practice for the correct path and really find the true taste of the path of practice.

When you practice again in the world of opposites, you will truly find yourself and truly know who you are. At the same time, this path of practice will rescue others from suffering.

This is the true path of Social Buddhism.

258. February 3, 1993. Honolulu

Daily life is very complicated and gives you a lot of headaches. But when the direction of your path is clear, no matter how many difficulties and headaches you have, life goes very well and without hindrances, especially if your path is for practice.

The path of practice always eliminates hindrances and blockages. But if you choose the path of greediness and desire, though it seems to be going well in the beginning, there is difficulty in the end. The path of practice is difficult in the beginning, but in the end it is bright and clear; you have no hindrances.

Human beings come into this world to attain the truth; that is our purpose in being here. We are not here only for bread and butter. Our duty and function is to be with the truth beyond form, so we will have infinite truth and infinite life. That is why we are here.

When many difficulties and headaches occur, drop everything and only concentrate on practice. Then everything will appear very smoothly and in the proper order.

259. February 4, 1993. Honolulu

Living in the O is a fearless life.

When you attain cause and effect and do not get caught by them, you can live a fearless life. At the same time, when you make your own cause and effect, if you know what you are doing, it is just like you are putting your life in your own palm. At that time, you can see your own life so clearly that you can create your life the way you want it to be, without fears. That is living in the clear O life.

What is not being caught by cause and effect?

Hi! May I help you?

260. February 5, 1993. Honolulu

The person who is able to make others comfortable has confidence in himself. The person who makes others uncomfortable and bothers them does not have confidence in himself.

The person who gets caught by perfectionism always bothers others. But the person who wants to make others comfortable and happy does not get caught by either perfectionism or neglectfulness. Such a person is always able to make others comfortable and happy.

Do not verify or check too much. While you are verifying and checking, at that moment you are bothering others and making yourself insecure. But if you only want to work for others and make them happy without verifying or checking, you will accomplish everything smoothly, without doubts. At that moment you are making yourself confident, secure and happy.

Make yourself round. Being sharp means poking yourself and others.

261. February 6, 1993. Honolulu

A rabbit was walking around on the mountain. All of a sudden he felt the whole mountain shaking. He was so surprised and scared, and he had no idea what was causing the shaking. Then he saw that a big tiger was walking.

The rabbit became amazed at the tiger's strength and scary form. At the same time, he wished he was like the tiger. He wanted to be bigger than a tiger.

He went home and told his wife, "Today, when I went to the mountain I saw a tiger, and I defeated him." The rabbit's wife had some doubts, but because her husband insisted it was true, she tried to believe him.

While they were having that conversation, some ants were listening and began laughing at the rabbit. The rabbit said, "Who do you think you are? Why are you laughing at me?" The ants said, "Do not try to show off how strong you are. Do not envy the strength of the tiger, and do not look down at us just because we are small. We can show you that we are stronger than a tiger."

A couple of days later, two tigers got into a fight and one of them died. At that time, all of the ants got together, brought the tiger into the ants' house and made a big party. The rabbit saw this and was amazed by the ants' action and by the mind and power of their getting together.

Striving mind and power transcend you and I to realize one mind. That one mind can move anything and can get anything.

The rabbit was deeply amazed and felt very ashamed for being individualistic and arrogant.

262. February 7, 1993. Honolulu

There is a mind which, when someone says to go east, wants to go west. It is a mind which, when someone says not to do something, wants to do it—a mind which always wants to argue with others. Find what that mind is and why it behaves like this.

Sentient beings are just like crying babies. Buddhas and bodhisattvas are just like a mother who calms down the crying babies and wants to give them everything they want.

263. February 8, 1993. Honolulu

An unwise person likes to have an explanation one hundred times, but yet he does not understand. A wise person asks a question once, receives a single explanation and already understands. An awakened person, with one blink of the eye, understands the question, the answer and everything.

But Buddhas and bodhisattvas give explanations one hundred times to the person who wants an explanation one hundred times. Also, if the person wants an explanation 1,000 times, they give an explanation 1,000 times. But if the person still does not understand, even if they give an explanation 10,000 times, the Buddha and bodhisattvas explain with compassionate tears.

264. February 9, 1993. Honolulu

Today is Ji Jang Bo Sal's day.

Be thankful to the ancestors who made your parents.

Be thankful to your parents who made you come to this world.

Be thankful to the teacher or master who has taught you.

Be thankful to your husband or wife, and to your family and friends.

Be thankful to all the people with whom you have had relations.

Apologize to the people with whom you have had very bad relations.

Also, take this self vow: 'From now on, I really will make good relations with everybody.'

265. February 10, 1993. Honolulu

Put the delusion which makes you go far away into this present form. Put that delusion into your black point • and think. Put that thinking into this moment, which is to put it into what is in front of you, such as 'see the carpet is red.'

The moment when your thinking is concentrated on the carpet and becomes one with the mind seeing the carpet, delusion is disappearing. Place this undeluded mind in beautiful thinking and repeat three times: "Today, no matter what kind of difficulty or ugly things appear, I will use my thinking and my mind beautifully."

266. February 11, 1993. Honolulu

Do not get caught by your thinking.

Do not be a slave of your thinking.

Become a master of your thinking.

If you get caught by your thinking, you will drown in your own illusion, lose yourself and become a puppet of others. When you become a slave of your thinking, even if you live a whole life, you do not know what this life is about, who you are or what true I is.

Until you become a master of your thinking, practice continuously. And when you find the master of your thinking, throw away that master and the thinking; just go.

Following that path, you will become one with the whole universe, become a great free person, make your own thinking and make your own master.

267. February 12, 1993. Los Angeles

When you plan for a business or the future, there are two different methods. The first is to think of your present situation as your roots: do not try to pull them out first in order to take them to another place. Rather, plant other roots first and let them grow. When those roots have settled and have grown very well, then the first roots which you had may be moved to where the new roots are.

The second method is to leave the roots as they are, keep them as a center and let new roots spread and branch out from there.

268. February 13, 1993. Paris

When you lower your head, you can obtain ten different things. When you keep your head stiffly, you lose ten different things. The head which is lowered kills I-my-me and at the same time makes others happy. This is the correct function of true I.

Unwise people always feel good when others lower their heads down to them. But when others lower their heads before a wise person, the wise person appreciates their humility and sincerity, and so lowers his or her head as well.

When you are able to lower own head, no matter how many difficult situations and blockages there are, you can pass through them very smoothly. But when you keep your head stiffly, you will lose yourself, and you will suffer from difficulties and blockages.

269. February 14, 1993. Paris

Check yourself to see that you really know what love is about. Do you only know conditional love, or do you know what unconditional love is?

Even if you love unconditionally, check to see if you have hindrances or no hindrance.

If you have hindrances, practice to eliminate them. And if you see that there is no hindrance, that means your path is getting deeper.

If you have someone to love unconditionally and without any hindrance, that is the greatest happiness. With that happiness you can create life as you wish and live an unhindered life.

If you truly attain love and know what it is about, you become love. With that love you can really give love to others and teach them what love is about.

270. February 15, 1993. Paris

When you are in a difficult situation, always force yourself to go in a positive direction. When you force yourself to go in a positive direction, all of the difficulties disappear and your situation becomes positive.

After your situation becomes positive, you become a friend of difficulty, and all the scars you got from your difficulties disappear.

271. February 16, 1993. Paris

Each human being lives in his own world but does not even know what his individual world is. So, how can people expect someone else to understand them?

People often get angry because others do not understand them. But, if you want someone else to understand you, first see and understand what your own world is about.

When you really know what your own world is, the expectation that someone else will understand you disappears. And at the same time, you are reluctant for anyone else to know you. You then want to eliminate the I that you know, and in order to do so you want to help others and put your energy into them. Then you will finally realize that others' happiness is actually the basis of your own true happiness.

272. February 17, 1993. Paris

When you have an important plan, do not attach to it. Before you put it into action, check that plan once again. Will it be a success or a failure?

If, for example, you first thought that this plan will succeed, but upon checking it you are doubtful that it will, discern clearly whether this plan is only for your own desire or purpose. If this plan is for others, it will bring benefit for others and will make them happy.

When you realize that, do not think about whether it will be a success or a failure; just do it without doubting.

273. February 18, 1993. Paris

Human beings' minds are all the same, but how they individually use this mind is different. They use their minds according to their individual karma - in a good way, in a bad way, in a pokey way, in a scratchy way or in a round way.

The path of human beings' minds coming together and becoming one mind is not to get caught by one's individual use of the mind. If you get caught by that you will lose yourself.

If you do not want to get caught by your individual use of the mind, do not insist upon your own opinion. Have great patience for listening to others' opinions; this great patience will lead to truly understanding others. If you truly understand others, you will not get caught by their opinions, and, at the same time, you will understand their original mind.

When you understand others' original mind, this original mind becomes one with your own original mind. This mind is beyond karma, is true human mind, and becomes one with the absolute, universal mind.

274. February 19, 1993. Paris

Those who know who they are never get caught by right and wrong and never check for right or wrong; they act freely and make others very comfortable, like warm sunshine.

Those who do not know who they are, in order to find themselves and know themselves, always check for right and wrong; they get caught by right and wrong.

In order to escape being caught by right and wrong, encroaching upon others' time and space, bothering others, becoming a nuisance to others and making yourself lonely, please practice vigorously and aim to become a comfortable person so that others can be at ease with you.

275. February 20, 1993. Paris

Knowing how to respect others means that your path is getting deeper and that your ego has disappeared.

Those who do not have ego create the karma of respecting others and always receive respect from others. Those who receive respect from others know who and what they are. Because they know who and what they are, they do want to show off. Even though they do not show off, however, they always shine and others always respect them. When such people receive respect from others, they are always appreciative, and with that appreciation strive to serve others.

In order to have such respect yourself, practice and try to respect others from now on, no matter who they are.

276. February 21, 1993. Paris

When you keep your vows and live life according to them, all of your delusions and devils disappear, and you are led to the path of wisdom. Those who keep their vows can eliminate all enticements and rescue themselves.

In this world, a lot of blockages and enticements are encountered while living everyday life. To be free of them all, leading yourself to the path of enlightenment and rescuing yourself from karma, is to go onto the path of keeping your vows and precepts and living according to them.

Live your life just like a lotus flower which is not dirtied by the filthy water in which it grows.

277. February 22, 1993. Paris

Let us live beautifully. Beauty comes from transcending the world of opposites, from transcending the world of doubting, and from always trusting and helping each other.

When you have a lot of doubts, you always check for right and wrong and say too much. When you say too much, you generate too many questions. Then even the Buddha cannot answer all your concerns.

Even if you are only saying one word, say it softly, accurately and concisely, respecting others. And even though you have doubts, speak softly and considerately, respecting others' opinions.

With the softly spoken single sentence, let us bring about a beautiful fragrance and let us have beautiful communication.

P. S. This teaching is very important

278. February 23, 1993. Paris

The 'no I' receives form with an existing karma. That form forgets the 'no I' and only remembers and believes in the karma I. Also, while this body (form) lives, it only respects and has faith in that karma I, so it always insists upon its own thinking and opinion. When the 'no I' sees this, it feels ridiculous and terrible, wishing that the karma I would disappear. The 'no I' waits for that to happen, but when the karma I is too strong, the 'no I' punishes it once in a while; then the karma I is surprised and wakes up from its darkness. Finally, it asks itself the big questions: "Who am I? What am I?"

While you are asking yourself this kind of question, forget everything and put everything down. This is the great path of becoming one with the 'no I.'

279. February 24, 1993. Paris

Life is coming here and going back to where we came from. Even though we go back to the same (original) place, while existing here, through our form, the traces of our thinking and actions always exist without disappearing. So when this form goes back to the original place, it cannot go freely because these traces always follow it, and it becomes a slave to them. Then, when these traces call, you go back to where they are calling from.

While living in this world, leave beautiful traces; then when these beautiful traces call you, you will come back to a beautiful place.

These beautiful traces will lead you to becoming a Buddha. When coming and going, that Buddha does not leave any traces and comes and goes freely.

280. February 25, 1993. Paris

The Korean phrase, *il chun o*, means turn your thinking around one more time.

If you think that you are right, but others do not agree with you, do not insist on your opinion. Rather, turn your thinking around one more time. When you do so, your ego disappears and you find out more clearly what others want. Then you can make them happy.

When you turn your thinking around one more time, that thinking is actually for others. So even though you do not insist upon your opinion, others will trust you and agree with your opinion.

When someone asks something of those who know *il chun o* or wants something from them, they do not say "no." Instead, they say, "I'll try my best."

Il chun o means bodhisattva action.

281. February 26, 1993. Paris

Trust the Buddha (absolute energy).

Trust the teachings.

Trust the practice.

This is the path of trusting yourself. If you can trust yourself, you can conquer any difficulty.

When you can conquer any difficulty, trust yourself. When you can trust yourself, thank the Buddha, thank the teachings, thank the practice, and thank the person who gave you a difficult situation.

282. February 27, 1993. Barcelona

Between Shakyamuni Buddha's form and our human being's form, there is no difference. Eyes, ears, nose, mouth, body, mind—everything is the same. So why did Shakyamuni became a Buddha while we human beings are still in the sentient beings' world? Think about it.

Shakyamuni Buddha realized the place of the mind, what the mind is, and how to use this mind correctly; through this, he realized incalculable wisdom. This wisdom became one with the absolute world and then became incalculable, supernatural penetration power.

That is why, even though he had the same human body, he became a Buddha.

As long as we human beings practice to know what the place of the mind is and realize what this mind is, we then become Buddhas, too.

Our daily teaching is the teaching of realizing the place of the mind and knowing how to use the mind. That is why they call this method "Dharma." By depending upon the Dharma and practicing it, one becomes a Buddha oneself.

We call the house where the Dharma is taught "Dharma Sah." Take care of each Dharma Sah just like your own body and strive to keep it clean and beautiful, just like your mind, so that many people may come and receive the teachings and protection.

283. February 28, 1993. Barcelona

The great Mount Sumeru is not higher than true I. An alfalfa seed is small, but cannot be smaller than true I. When true I goes to the mountain, it becomes a tree; when true I goes to the ocean, it becomes a fish; when true I goes to the land, it becomes a human being. This I, when you put it in a big box, will fill it; when you put it in a small box, it fits perfectly.

This I does not have name, does not have form. Our human form cannot see this I. This human form typically wants to run away elsewhere and ends up drowning in hell. But when this form sees that the sky is blue, the carpet is red, and correctly hears the sound of the bird, it becomes one with this true I, does together-action with this I, and then, wherever this form goes, it makes a paradise and happiness.

284. March 1, 1993 Barcelona.

Two thousand five hundred and thirty-seven years ago, Shakamuni Buddha wanted to know what is inside of the spider web and what is outside of the spider web. Because he wanted to realize that, he left his home 2,537 years ago, today.

After six years of ascetic practice, he found the true I which is outside of the spider web. With that true I and wisdom he found that, even if you live inside of the spider web, you can have a happy, tranquil and comfortable life. So he came back into the spider web again and with his wisdom showed us correct methods of going through this spider-web life.

Until today, we use his wisdom and methods of practice, and so inside the spider web becomes brighter and his teachings shine eternally.

We should be thankful to Shakyamuni Buddha, who had a great vow and intention to save all sentient beings. Let us be especially thankful for his teachings.

285. March 2, 1993. Barcelona

When you are able to differentiate between karma I and true I, then you can correctly enter the path of Buddha. True I always watches the karma I—observing what it is thinking and how it is acting. It always watches.

The true I always stays in the bright, clear, comfortable and tranquil place. So when there is a comfortable, tranquil and beautiful place, the true I goes there and provides you with everything you need and makes you happy.

In our human mind there is the karma I and the true I. So people often find that they have two different personalities. But there are not two different personalities. Because in our mind we have one side which is karma I and one side which is true I, we think that we have two different personalities.

When you feel very uncomfortable, angry, depressed and negative, it is your karma I which is doing it. At that time, immediately think about the bright and comfortable side, which will eliminate your karma I and place you in the true I.

So always strive and practice to put yourself into the true I. This is the practice to become a Buddha.

286. March 3, 1993. Paris

Those who do not know love are always dry in speech, action and thinking; they are always bothering others and making them suffer. Those who know love, even though their speech, action and thinking are rough, are always making others comfortable and happy.

Karma I does not have love; it only has ego. True I love always flows, is humble and lives for others.

Practice sincerely and vigorously, eliminate karma I and find true I, so you can receive respect and love from others and give them true love. At the same time, be thankful for love. Always be happy, tranquil and comfortable, and relax.

287. March 4, 1993. Paris

Do you see this bright and clear place? Do you see this empty place which is the O place? The sky is blue, the carpet is red. Do you see? Is it clear?

Now, do not get caught by 'the sky is blue' or 'the carpet is red.' Transcend 'the sky is blue,' 'the carpet is red.' Can you see that emptiness which transcends 'sky is blue, the carpet is red'? Can you see?

If you say you can see, you are wrong; if you say you cannot see, you are still wrong. Then what is this?

Rinzai Zen Master, do not make this place noisy with your KATZ. Mahakasapa, do not influence this place with your smile. Un Chung Zen Master, do not make this place stinky with your dry shit on a stick. Guji Zen Master, do not stick your finger out towards this place; you will get hurt.

Then what is this??

March 3, 1993, 7:00AM, 1 minute, 3 seconds... drawing a single lotus flower on the white paper. Ahhh! Beautiful! Wonderful! Thank you very much!!

P. S. This is a very important teaching. Read it over and over again and try to attain it.

P. P. S. Mahakasapa was the Buddha's first disciple to receive transmission, when he smiled as the Buddha held up a flower before a large assembly on Yong San Mountain. Rinzai Zen Master, Un Chung Zen Master and Guji Zen Master were great Chan masters from China, each of whom had trademark methods of teaching to explain the true place. Rinzai Master always let out a "KATZ," the great Zen shout. Un Chung Master's "dry shit on a stick" became a famous teaching when, while one day cleaning a toilet with a stick, he gave that reply to a student's question, "What is Buddha?" To any question asked him, Guji Master answered by sticking out one finger.

288. March 5, 1993. Paris

When you are in a dark cloud, you see everything as dark, you think in a dark way, and you even do not know what kind of speech and action you are making; you do not realize it. At the same time, you are bothering others and making them suffer, but you do not realize that you are doing so.

Practice vigorously, exit the dark cloud and enter the path of clarity. The method of coming out from the dark cloud is, when someone scolds you or complains about you, and you become very angry, immediately see that angry mind. That anger is actually your karma from your last life that you have carried into the present.

When you realize that karma, promise yourself you will not repeat it. At the same time, appreciate the person who complained about you or who scolded you, try to understand others, and present a love mind to everybody. That love mind is connected to your truth, which will prevent you from going into the dark cloud again.

289. March 6, 1993. Dorsten

Satisfy your present life now. Satisfy your present situation now. Satisfy your present relationships now, and do not discriminate between good and bad.

Appreciate everything unconditionally and rest assured that you are the happiest person in the world.

Repeat each of the following sentences 108 times:

"I am happy." "I am satisfied." "I am bright."

Be like a lotus flower which, without words, blooms and wilts in the dirty water.

290. March 7, 1993. Dorsten

After you come into this world, the greatest happiness is when you can go back, one hundred percent. If, because of your karma, you cannot leave one hundred percent, that is suffering.

Today is Buddha's Nirvana Day, which is the day he left one hundred percent. He came into this world, he emptied himself out, he gave all of himself to others, and he gave us teaching about how to empty out ourselves and how to help others. Then he left one hundred percent, 2,537 years ago, today.

When you are here in this world, throw away your three poisons, which are greed, anger and ignorance. Then, you live only to make others happy; you live only to make others comfortable; you live only to help others.

Then, when we leave this world, we can have true, happy nirvana. And when we come back to this world again, we come absolutely freely. We can come and go as we wish and, in the footprints of our coming and going, lotus flowers will bloom and make everybody happy.

291. March 8, 1993. Dorsten

Even in a diamond there is a flaw (*teakkl*). When there is not a flaw, the color is not perfect. Even in the absolute energy, which is very clear, very beautiful, very clean and very bright, there was a flaw (*teakkl*). Because of that flaw (*teakkl*), this universe and our planet appeared; the mountains, oceans and so on appeared; and then human beings appeared.

Especially for human beings, our original ancestor was the flaw (*teakkl*). We human beings were originally made from this flaw (*teakkl*), and that is why we are not perfect. But because human beings are not perfect, they always have a yearning to be perfect, always yearn to be right and always yearn to be correct.

If you really want to be perfect, do not get caught by this flaw (*teakkl*); find the true, absolute world which is beyond the *teakkl*, which is to find the O. In the O, there is bright wisdom. With this wisdom, whether there is a *teakkl* or not, you can overlook everything, without being hindered. With this wisdom, you do not get caught by the *teakkl* and at the same time you know how to take care of this *teakkl* and how to make it happy. With that *teakkl*, you can realize your true self.

If you want to be perfect, do not get caught by perfectionism and do not suffer by discriminating between right and wrong. Such discrimination makes both you and others suffer. And just because you are greedy about becoming perfect, do not become angry and do not act ignorantly. Remember: our ancestors were imperfect and were mistakes.

P. S. The *teakkl* is a flaw, an imperfection and a mistake.

P. P. S. Read this teaching over and over again.

292. March 9, 1993. Paris

To everybody,

I love you all very much.
Ji Kwang

293. March 10, 1993. Paris

Let us not live a headache life.

Let us not live a suffering life.

Give an inch to others. When you give an inch to others, you do not get a headache and you do not suffer. But when you hold onto thinking you are right, when you hold onto your intelligence, and when you try to take someone else's inch away, you get a headache and you suffer.

So give an inch to each other. Then both you and others will be happy.

Do not take away. Give. When you take away, you suffer. When you give, you become happy.

294. March 11, 1993. Paris

When wisdom light shines, it illuminates even the darkest cave and makes it bright; it brings everything into view. But when you are in ignorance, you cannot see, and so your mind becomes at ease and does not do a lot of thinking. But when you can see everything, your mind is not at ease and a lot of thinking appears. At this time, is wisdom light better or is ignorance better? Try to judge which one is better.

Wisdom light, which is not at ease and does a lot of thinking, becomes a lotus flower and makes others' minds beautiful and happy. But the ignorant mind, which is at ease and does not do a lot of thinking, becomes a poisonous mushroom and poisons others.

So would you like to be clear or would you like to be ignorant? Answer me!

295. March 12, 1993. Paris

When ants are in a group and work together, they always live and eat well. But if one ant thinks that it is 1, it leaves the group, disparages others and acts alone. At first, this ant seems to be very free and independent, but before long it gets caught by the spider's web and becomes spider food. But the group of ants can poke a hole and go through any kind of spider web.

Then, even the spider becomes frightened and runs away.

296. March 13, 1993. Munich

The soreness and scars that are inflicted by the beast, put them into the O.

At first they hurt a lot and caused a lot of suffering, but after being put into the O, these scars and soreness slowly disappeared, and the body and mind became comfortable. I felt a lot of pity for that angry and cold beast that hurt me and was sorry for it. At the same time, I had a lot of agony over how to make that beast into a Buddha. I concentrated so much on that task that I did not realize when day had gone and night had come; time and space became one. That oneness became wisdom light which shone upon everything and made everything bright and clear. The beast disappeared and even Buddha did too.

The flower on the table smiles at me quiescently. Without realizing it, I put my lips to the flower and I kisssssss! I love you!

P. S. This is a very important teaching for everyone.

297. March 14, 1993. Munich

Doing this way, so what?

Doing that way, so what?

Alps Mountains, stone lion, having a baby, so what?

You do not have to know how many baby lions the keen-eyed lion on Mount Sumeru has. If you do know, so what? If you do not know, so what?

But if you really want to know how the stone lion makes a baby, go into the lair of the keen-eyed lion on Mount Sumeru with gifts of toys for his baby lions. Then you will know.

P. S. What does this mean? Old students especially must answer this *kong-an*.

298. March 15, 1993. Munich

The flower is beautiful, but then you start fingering it to figure out why it bloomed the way it did and why it looks as it does. Because of your curiosity, you pull off one petal and look at it. But that one petal by itself is not beautiful. And by pulling off the petal, you cause the flower to suffer and lose its beauty.

Do not touch the flower. Just see its beauty as it is and be thankful for it. That mind which simply gazes at the flower's beauty just as it is also makes you beautiful and comfortable. Then that flower will give you an infinitely beautiful mind.

299. March 16, 1993. Munich

The Dharma arrow does not have sympathy or sentimentality. No matter whom it pierces, wherever there is delusion, wherever there is ignorance, the Dharma arrow flies directly there.

When you receive this arrow, do not become angry and do not suffer. This arrow eliminates your delusions and wakes you up from ignorance. So when this arrow comes to you, greet it happily and be thankful for it. At the same time, do not become depressed just because, still being in ignorance, you have a lot of delusion. At that moment, heal your scars with your practice. Practice is to transform being human from being imperfect to being perfect; it is making yourself a correct human and performing human beings' correct function.

300. March 17, 1993. Paris

In the round moon and in the pumpkin moon, there is a shadow. In the round moon's shadow, you make (drawing of a heart).

Take the pumpkin moon's pumpkin seeds, roast them very well, remove the shells one by one, and place these toasted seeds in your lover's mouth.

Doing is love.

Giving is love.

Buddha's great compassion and great love face is always round and bright.

301. March 18, 1993. Honolulu

When you are in this world, do not be dragged around by your karma I (karma I is your own condition, your own righteousness and your own opinion). Moment to moment, this karma I appears and confuses you.

Make this karma I your own and use it as your royal servant. When you can do that, your true I is always relaxed and comfortable and makes others happy. Remember, your karma I always causes separation from others, bothers others and makes them suffer.

So every moment, from time to time, see yourself; which one is your karma I, which one is your true I? *See that when someone else is truly comfortable and happy, that is your true I; when someone else is not happy, that is your karma I.* The reason is that inside the absolute truth is the most comfortable, most tranquil place, without differentiation and discrimination.

P. S. What does the italicized phrase mean to you?

302. March 19, 1993. Honolulu

In our stressful life, our ears only hear complaints and our heads only think about how to defend ourselves from those complaints, how to defeat and be better than others, and how to show off that we are better than they are. Our heads are full of these kinds of thoughts. Also, at this very moment as you are reading this sentence, you want to deny and disagree with it.

So, to try to transcend the opposites-world and to go into the true I world, open your ears to the birds singing in the morning and to the sounds of the wind blowing at night.

303. March 20, 1993. Honolulu

Coming into this world is not easy. Leaving this world is also not easy.

If you really attain this, get away from suffering as soon as possible.

Normally our life is ninety percent suffering and ten percent happiness. But most people do not even have this ten percent of happiness.

So practice people: change this. Put ninety percent into happiness and do not think of the other ten percent as suffering. Think of that ten percent as resources for your practice to become better. Also, make your life a graceful life, which means speaking gracefully, acting gracefully and thinking gracefully. This is making your life one hundred percent happy. Then, when you leave this world, you will go away gracefully and without regret.

P. S. Find your own methods for thinking gracefully. This is very important. Discuss it.

304. March 21, 1993. Honolulu

When you are in the karma world, even if you have a friend, it is not a true relationship. When you make a friend in the conditional world, if you do not receive some benefit for yourself, you do not take him or her as a friend. Also, you fear that you are being used by others and so you put yourself inside a thick turtle shell. This is why it is difficult to have a true friendship.

But when your karma slowly disappears, your turtle shell, conditions and expectations disappear. You begin thinking about how you can help your friends more and how you can make them happy.

Also, you appreciate that you have friends whom you can help and at the same time you appreciate your friends who accept your help. When you can do this, you can live life appreciatively and richly, without being lonely.

305. March 22, 1993. Honolulu

Body suffering, mind suffering: people cannot keep these sufferings to themselves; they always want to share them with others. Those who do this do not know what suffering is, and that is why they make others suffer.

Because some people grew up in suffering they think that suffering is correct, and so they give suffering to others. But when someone does not want to receive that suffering, he or she becomes very angry. At that time, those who grew up in suffering realize what suffering is about, but even so they will not try to eliminate it and will try to go more deeply into it.

This is just like people who are afraid of coming out of the dark cloud; when they see the sunshine, they are afraid and so they burrow more deeply into the cloud and believe that the cloud is the truth.

P. S. Everyone please think seriously about this subject.

306. March 23, 1993. Honolulu

How you use energy determines how your life is. Arrogant people who always doubt about others and think about how good they are always use energy in a very negative way. But people who do not have any attachments and who know how to live happily, moment-to-moment, always use energy in a positive way and always make others happy.

But if a positive person hangs around negative people, his or her energy will also become negative. So until you become clear, stay away from negative people and protect yourself. When you become clear and must deal with negative people, you deal with them in a negative way; and when you deal with positive people, you deal with them in a positive way. But you teach the negative person what compassion is, and you show and give the positive person great love.

307. March 24, 1993. Honolulu

Even if you have suffering in the body, this suffering is not only for yourself. It is to make beauty and to make others happy. If you realize this, you do not call it "suffering," you call it the correct function of this form.

Remember, in the O there is no you or I; we always exist here. So when others are suffering, we help them through the energy line; and when the suffering disappears, we make them very happy with our energy line practice. This is because we are an infinite family, together all of the time. Those who have the energy line: always remember that you are not alone.

308. March 24, 1993. Honolulu

In the street and even in the house there are many signs saying, "Do not do it, do not do it." These signs are there because we are not clear. So everywhere we go, restrictions are placed on us.

But if everyone finds who they are, we will not have these kinds of signs. Instead, wherever we go, all the signs will say, "Please be happy here. I make a comfortable place for you. Enjoy your life!" We will have these kinds of signs.

So from today, do not be enslaved by the signs that say, "Do not do this, do not do that." Just be comfortable, wherever you go.

309. March 25, 1993. Honolulu

When this body hurts, there is a reason. But often the mind does not have sympathy for the body and blames it, "Why do you hurt?"

The body without mind is not a body; the mind without a body or form is not a mind. So, when the mind which is not mind meets the form, it does not see itself and is caught by the form, becomes a slave to it and makes a lot of karma. And when form without form meets the mind, it does not see itself and only uses the mind to make very bad karma.

When form knows mind and mind knows form, at that time they come together, take care of one another and live happily together.

310. March 26, 1993. Honolulu

This form is here in this world now; so think about what you would like to do with it. This form always loses its correct function because of delusions and fantasies. So if this form wants to get away from delusions and fantasies, always think about what you are going to do with it now. Is it making others happy now, or is it bothering others? Always think about what you are going to do with this present form now.

When you are aware of this, you will go onto the correct path of life and will keep this form correctly during its entire existence.

311. March 27, 1993. Honolulu

Always put this body into the O and give it a bath. Put everything—all delusions, ego and dirt—into the O and take a bath, day and night. The more you take a bath day and night, the more the body disappears and the mind disappears. Then, body becomes wisdom and mind becomes bright. Then, wherever you go and whoever you are with, ignorance disappears and everything becomes beautiful.

P. S. Today is a day when the body needs energy. So eat very well. Eat up well!!!

312. March 28, 1993. Honolulu

When you come into this world, there are a lot of things to see and hear, and everything is so big that it overwhelms you. Those who have a lot of karma are always caught by those many things and want to have them all. Such people are drowning in the world, suffering, and have a difficult time getting out.

But those who have practiced from last life are born into this world with bodhisattva karma. So when they come into this world they do not attach to or want many things. They just take something when needed and know how to be satisfied with what they have, living meaningfully and creatively every day.

The practice person's present practice leads him or her to the bodhisattva path in this life and in the next life, too.

313. March 29, 1993. Honolulu

When you do not know your true self, everything seems to be blocked and everything seems to be a hindrance. When you try to get away from blockages and hindrances, you irritate yourself and others, blaming others for everything and making everything unhappy. When you try to find happiness, it is almost impossible.

But when you know your true self, there are no blockages or hindrances, and everything becomes very comfortable and beautiful. When there is a difficulty, you see it as an interesting experience. So no matter what difficulty appears, you are always in happiness.

In the eyes of those who have found the truth, everything seems to be round; in their ears, all noise is heard as music; in their noses, everything has the fragrance of a flower; the speech coming out of their mouths always makes others happy; and wherever they go, whatever they do always shines and makes others comfortable and happy.

314. March 30, 1993. Honolulu

A caterpillar becomes a butterfly. Until the butterfly can fly freely there are a lot of changes. It is just like when going from ignorance into the clear world—there are many levels to pass through.

So while you are practicing, there are many changes in yourself and you will be surprised. Let those changes come naturally, and do not hold onto the past and do not attach to your past experiences. If you attach to past experiences, you are not going through the correct levels. Just have an experience and then forget about it, and do not be afraid of what comes next. And do not indulge in your interesting experiences; just let them go. Then, when you reach the clear world, everything you experienced is going to help others.

Remember, the butterfly goes here and there, to this and that flower, makes them happy and transmits love and truth to each flower.

315. March 31, 1993. Honolulu

If you want to be happy and successful, first fill in where you are lacking and fix your complexes. Strive to do this, always doing your best. But if you have difficulty filling your lacks and fixing your complexes, forget about them until you cannot even think about them anymore.

Striving to fill in your lacks and fix your complexes is to make yourself happy and successful. Happiness and success do not come from outside.

P.S. What are you lacking and what are your complexes? Find those things now.

316. April 1, 1993. Honolulu

The rougher nature energy becomes, the rougher humans' minds become. Then, human beings only like rough things, talk and act roughly and only look for rough experiences, such as violent movies. All of these things make them rougher.

Dear practitioner, do not get caught by this kind of situation. Find peace and tranquility within the noise and find beauty within the roughness. Without being caught by any situation, find the bright clarity in the O and live everyday clearly.

317. April 2, 1993. Honolulu

Today, contemplate your dharma name. Your dharma name carries your duty, what you must do in this life. So think about how you can accomplish that duty one hundred percent. This is just like the role given to an actor or actress by the director; when the actor or actress does an excellent job, he or she wins an Oscar.

Practice person, when you do the duty of your dharma name one hundred percent, you will get the absolute-world-supernatural-penetration-power award. So strive to do the duty of your dharma name one hundred percent. This is the correct path to eliminate one's karma and to go from the world of ignorance to the world of clarity. In the world of clarity, create life's true beauty, infinitely.

318. April 3, 1993. Honolulu

The Human Path

> In the place which does not have name and form,
> Name and form appear.
> Name and form fight each other, win and lose.
> When loss, sadness.
> When victory, happiness.
> Without predictions, without saying, one day name suddenly disappears, form disappears.
> Only the trace which is hanging on the name is left.
> Suddenly one day, appear with shoes on that are the same size as the trace.
> And then, with those shoes on, again running around.

> Ahha!...Your shoes are small...My shoes are big...Your shoes are ugly...My shoes are nice looking...Ha Ha Ha Ha!!

P. S. Meditate very seriously upon this.

319. April 4, 1993. Honolulu

A tired body makes more delusion. A healthy body makes more desire.

Make the tired body relax so that delusion also relaxes. And make the healthy body busy so that desire quickly disappears.

But a clear person, whether healthy or tired, does not get caught by body conditions. Clear people know how to use their body correctly from moment to moment. This is just like a horse rider who knows when to pull tightly on the horse's reins and when to loosen them.

320. April 5, 1993. Honolulu

To stop the baby from crying, you put all of your effort into giving him what he wants. And to try to help the sick baby, you do not sleep or even think about your own body; you only try to help the sick baby.

If you do these kinds of actions and have this kind of mind towards your family, friends, teachers and everybody whom you know, then you will become a bodhisattva yourself and you will be treated as a Buddha by others.

321. April 6, 1993. Honolulu

I must realize that I am others. When I only do for myself and I only think about myself, then I do not know myself.

When I understand others and when I think about others, then I know myself.

[Today, everybody think about Dae Poep Sa Nim and make 108 prostrations in front of her photo. Then sit and repeat the mantra for ten minutes and see yourself and what you realize.]

322. April 7, 1993. Honolulu

Today, live one hundred percent in love. Put all of your delusions, agonies and difficulties into love.

Delusions, agonies and difficulties cause the body and mind pain. So put everything into love.

Today, whoever you meet, whether they are good or difficult people, deal with them with love and say, "I love you!"

323. April 8, 1993. Honolulu

Today is the day of freedom—free from delusions, agonies and blockages, and especially free from karma. So put down whatever you have been holding in your mind, for example, bad thinking, hateful thinking and difficult thinking. Put it all down and free yourself. At that moment, you can become one with the absolute, you can really have a taste of the truth, and you can put yourself into the true world.

Live truthfully all day today; speak truthfully, think truthfully and act truthfully. Spend the day truthfully, one hundred percent.

324. April 9, 1993. Honolulu

Time is always flowing. When born, then getting old; once old, going back to whence you came.

Nobody is special; everyone is the same. But while living in this world, the person who does not get angry, is not greedy, does not hurt others, is not jealous of others, and only loves and wants to help others has a special situation.

As such people get older, they shine more. When they go back whence they came, they are very comfortable. Whenever they are reborn, they are always comfortable. They are not hindered by coming and going. These are absolutely free people.

325. April 10, 1993. Honolulu

Remember your past difficulties and be satisfied with your present situation. Do not forget that there will be happiness in the future. Practice person, when you look at the past, present and future, you can see that as time goes by life gets continuously better and better.

Practicing people's time is always interesting. As time goes by they understand themselves and realize how to use themselves. When you realize how to use yourself, you will know the value of life. When you know the value of life, everyday life is so interesting, day by day.

326. April 11, 1993. Honolulu

In the universe, I exists.
In the I, the universe exists.

The I which knows that the universe exists in the I does not have name and form. This I has supernatural penetration power which has no name, no form.

This I makes everything, keeps everything alive and exists eternally. This is why our human body exists: to find this I. When this body finds this I, we call that body a Buddha and a bodhisattva body. This Buddha and bodhisattva body always appears according to cycles and situations, and wherever this body goes and stays, it always teaches others in order for them to become Buddha and bodhisattva bodies themselves.

Whether one person, one hundred or ten thousand people become Buddhas and bodhisattvas, without calculating, Buddha and bodhisattva bodies continuously appear in this world and teach until all sentient beings become Buddhas and bodhisattvas. It does not matter how long that takes, whether it is one hundred or ten thousand years.

327. April 12, 1993. Honolulu

Because you want to earn many things, you put a lot of energy into that. But just because you earn only a little bit, do not be disappointed. That little bit becomes a seed which will enable you to earn a lot. So do not disparage that little bit; appreciate what you have earned and at the same time strive to keep it.

Remember, when you earn one, you can earn ten thousand; and when you lose one, you can lose ten thousand.

328. April 13, 1993. Honolulu

The Buddha's smiling face is always bright and clear. But an ignorant person sees that face as angry and sad. Where does that anger and sadness go? They return to the person who made them. When you see the Buddha's face as happy and satisfied, where does that luck go to? It returns to you. And if, just because the Buddha always smiles, you treat him lightly and with arrogance, where does that go?

Think about all of this and see your actions, thinking and speech.

329. April 14, 1993. Honolulu

When negative thinking appears, do not feel bad about it and do not try to analyze why it has appeared, what it means, and what it will bring in the future. Do not get caught by such thinking. Throw away that negative thinking right away and repeat three times, "This negative thinking is not my thinking. This does not belong to me." See the floor in front of you, see the sky, and do what you must do in this moment.

Remember, life is always interesting and affords us many things to do. So do not waste time on negative thinking that does not bring you anything.

P. S. Today is a day when one can easily get caught by negative thinking.

330. April 15, 1993. Honolulu

The greatest happiness is when you have someone whom you can truly help, one hundred percent.

The greatest happiness is also when you can give everything that you have to that person, without feeling worn out or that you have lost something.

The greatest happiness is also when you have someone whom you help one hundred percent, but you do not even think that you have helped him.

When what you do is only for your own benefit, you always get caught by the world of opposites. But when what you do is for others, no matter how much difficulty appears, you can overcome the difficulty and success always follows.

331. April 16, 1993. Honolulu

Today is a day of frugality and moderation. So be moderate in whatever you want today. Eat only fifty percent, spend only fifty percent, be angry only fifty percent, be depressed only fifty percent, be happy only fifty percent and save the other fifty percent that is left over.

But love one hundred percent.

332. April 17, 1993. Honolulu

Ten thousand dharmas go back to one. But if that one is not clear and wise, those 10,000 dharmas are not clear and wise.

So, do not be confused by trying to follow 10,000 dharmas. Keep that one, and make that one become bright and clear. Then this bright and clear one makes 10,000 dharmas bright and clear, which make everything happy and bright.

And then, when these bright and clear 10,000 dharmas go back to one, that one is not caught by oneness. That bright and clear one then makes 10,000 dharmas beautiful.

333. April 18, 1993. Kyoto.

In Kyoto, Japan, the houses are so tightly packed together that there is not any wide space; the city is so full, it is just like a bee house. When you look at it, it seems as if there is not even room to breathe and that it must be so uncomfortable.

But even though there is this kind of situation, when you are looking for the truth in such a place, simply act in accord with ethics and local manners, caring for and respecting each other. If you live like this, you will not encounter loneliness, you will not find laziness, and negative emotions cannot exist.

Even though the land is as small as the palm of a hand, you can transform that small land into a block of gold and make each other Buddha.

So whether an environment is wide or narrow, practicing people are not hindered by anything and can always live correctly in an absolutely free life.

334. April 19, 1993. Kyoto

Good memory, bad memory, I have already put them down, so there are no hindrances. When I meet an old friend again I am so happy and thankful for his presence. But that old friend did not put it down, is caught by memory. Even if I ask to meet him, he is angry and runs away. It is pitiful.

While you are living here in this world, you put everything down so that when you die and are reborn again, there are no hindrances. But that friend would like to take everything with him to the other world and try to make a relationship again when he comes back. This must be a very deep relationship.

So I practice for him to be clear so that he can put it down and live comfortably, without hindrance. The day he becomes clear he will realize my true love for him. I hope it does not take too long.

335. April 20, 1993. Kyoto

In Kyoto, Japan, leaders from all over the world came together in one place. It is very interesting. Everyone is a leader and everyone's intention is to help all sentient beings. That intention is great, and we must have respect and appreciation for it.

Because all of these leaders did a lot of bodhisattva actions in their last lives, they became leaders this life. Being together with all of these bodhisattvas makes me happy. But these bodhisattvas have too many ideas and opinions and so they talk a lot. That obscures the blue sky.

So I made them hold hands with each other and practice together, saying: "*Na Mu Bul…*" Then the next moment we could see: the sky is blue, the wall is white. After that, I had them repeat three times, "How may I help you?" Now everyone is happy!

336. April 21, 1993. Kyoto

Those who can truly give themselves to others know what the truth is. Those who are always checking why they must give to others do not know what the truth is. And those who live only for themselves, for their own fame and to show off, do not know what the truth is.

Only those who do not think about themselves and who only live for others have attained what the truth is. Those who always think about others, research how to make them happy and comfortable, and who only live to do this, are the truth. No matter where such people go, they always save others, heal their mind sicknesses, their body sicknesses, and make everyone happy, showing them true beauty.

337. April 22, 1993. Kyoto

We are one family which lives on a single globe. But even though we live on the same globe, we do not know each other. Also, we do not even know our own selves.

Even though the same family meets together, we do not recognize each other. This is just like a mother who meets her own child but does not recognize that this person is her own child, or a child who meets his own parents but does not recognize that they are his own parents. This means that every individual lives in his own karma world, is attached to his own opinions and ideas, and in that small world thinks that he is the best. So how can the family harmonize? If we live without recognizing one another, how can this globe become comfortable? The globe was beautiful before. But now, because of human beings' ignorance, it has become weak and is losing its beauty. This is pitiful.

We human beings owe a huge debt to this globe. If we want to repay this debt, first we must realize who we are, what we are.

Becoming clear is very important. With clarity we can recognize our own family.

Family members respect and appreciate one another and share love together. Living thus, we can repay the debts we have to this globe and can make it beautiful. At the same time, this globe will protect us.

Doing so is the truly joyful life.

338. April 23, 1993. Honolulu

We human beings who live in the truth and love, if we really want to know what love and truth are, if we want to become one with the truth and live truly and lovingly, we must not be jealous. If you have jealousy, polish yourself to be bright and clear. And if someone is jealous of you, do not be hindered or disappointed. Deal with that person with love and truth. But if that person continues to be jealous of you, pause, wait and forget about it. Then the day will come when that person will know your love and truth.

Jealousy is the biggest blockage that keeps you away from happiness. Remember, if you are jealous, practice harder and become bright and clear.

339. April 24, 1993. Honolulu

When you are in difficult situations, close your ears, close your eyes, close your mouth and close your nose. Put your thinking into the Buddha (absolute energy) and put your action into practice. Just go forward. Then you can see the bright day which is right in front of your eyes.

P. S. Since 1990, this globe has been turning in an incorrect way. Scientists have now discovered that and many are very pessimistic about the future of our globe. But it will soon return to turning in the correct way. In the meantime, do not worry and live the way which is written about above.

340. April 25, 1993. Honolulu

Relax! Relax one hundred percent. Everybody is very tight, so relax.

341. April 26, 1993. Honolulu

In a relationship which comes from desire, when desire disappears, the relationship disappears.

In a relationship which comes from the truth, when desire appears, the relationship disappears. But if that was a true relationship, when the desire disappears, then true relationship comes back again.

But even in relationships that come from desire, if the partners would like to find the truth together and with that truth help others, and if their purposes are clear and they strive to achieve them and practice, then even desire can be turned into truth. Their relationship becomes a true relationship and they can live happily together, infinitely.

P. S. Think about what kind of relationship you have. Does it come from desire or from the truth?

342. April 27, 1993. Honolulu

SMILE!

Put all delusions into smiling. Smile for yourself; smile for others.

When a regular human being comes from his mother's stomach he comes out crying, lives sorrowfully in this world and, when he goes back, he goes back sorrowfully.

Practice people, how about changing this? Live with a smile, go with a smile. A true smile comes from non-hindrance. So find the non-hindrance place and attain Yong San Mountain's flower-smile. A true smile makes this whole globe beautiful. So always relay this true smile to others.

Just as a lion is not scared by any sound,

Just as the wind does not get caught by a net,

Just as the lotus flower is not soiled by the dirty water,

Go with a smile.

P. S. Yong San Mountain is where the Buddha held up a flower in front of a large assembly, and Mahakasapa, one of his disciples, smiled and thereupon received transmission from the Buddha.

343. April 28, 1993. Honolulu

Be bright and clear.

Look at the world like you are looking into a mirror.

When you can see this world as if in a mirror, do not get caught by what you see and do not get caught by the actions of others. Without getting caught, you can just see clearly and, at the same time, know how to respond clearly. Then this world is like a paradise. You will have a lot of fun here and can just go straight ahead, like the wind which does not get caught by a net.

Be clear and clear.

344. April 29, 1993. Honolulu

Buddha (absolute energy) is always protecting us, but we do not know what Buddha is and so we only want to protect ourselves. Doing so, we make everything difficult.

When we try to protect ourselves without knowing Buddha, our life is like a small boat in high waves. But when we know what Buddha is, when we have faith in and entrust everything to Buddha, our life is like a boat on the calm ocean.

That mind which knows what Buddha is and which trusts Buddha is the mind which can be one with Buddha. That one mind can conquer all difficulties and wants to love and protect everybody. With this one mind, no matter where you go, you will always receive love and respect from others.

As soon as possible, see the Buddha which is in front of your eyes. This Buddha is always waiting for you to see and recognize him.

345. April 30, 1993. Honolulu

From this mind to that mind; from here to there; always changing. This is human beings' mind and life; it is just like flowing water. But if flowing water gets caught by a valley and stays there too long, it becomes stagnant and unhealthy. Humans' minds are just like that.

So, no matter what happens or what kind of agonies you have, do not get caught by them. Find solutions to your problems while doing your daily jobs one hundred percent. Then, just like flowing water which has been stuck somewhere and begins flowing again, all your problems and agonies will be spontaneously solved.

What is your daily duty today?

346. May 1, 1993. San Francisco

When I want to know what I am, I first eliminate the desires that appear from my body.

As those desires disappear, one by one, it is just like clouds that have been obscuring the sky, disappearing one after another. My head, which was heavy, then becomes lighter. That lightened head makes the body and mind comfortable and without hindrance. The desires that I had then change into desires to help others.

Others' happiness is my happiness, and with that true happiness my life is without hindrance, and I live a truly happy life.

347. May 2, 1993. Paris

Going here and there, it is not only the body that moves. The mind is also moving.

If you watch that mind which is moving at the same time as the body, you see that it changes according to others and according to the situation.

When you can see the mind which changes, no matter who you meet or what kind of situation you are in, you will always know how to make the mind comfortable.

The mind that makes it comfortable for the mind which changes is your true I. Become the master of that mind which knows that true I and live brightly.

348. May 3, 1993. Paris

Even though you are clear, when others are not clear they can make you confused, unclear and uncomfortable. They can obscure your clarity, and that obscured mind easily turns into anger and blame, and makes unexpected karma.

At such times, do not blame others. Blame yourself for not being sufficiently clear, and practice harder to become absolutely clear; also, practice for those who make you unclear and uncomfortable.

Put your two hands together in hapchang; one hand is for you and one hand is for others.

349. May 4, 1993. Paris

When you make your mind small, your world becomes small. When you make your mind wide, your world becomes wide.

So do not get hung up on small little things, thus making your own world small; and do not attach to wideness, thus losing your own world.

Today, think about how to live appreciatively and stylishly and act accordingly. Then, your world will become appreciative and stylish. Act as if you are the most beautiful woman or handsome man in the world.

Put some beautiful color into your own world. Try it!

350. May 5, 1993. Puchberg, Austria

All things in the universe live in the absolute power. This absolute power creates everything and at the same time protects every little thing.

We human beings are also from this absolute power and live in it. But we attach only to our form and get caught by it, and we forget this absolute power and its protection, only following the conditions that appear from our form. This separates us from the absolute power and causes us to suffer unnecessarily.

Enlightenment means realizing this absolute power which is before form. Upon realizing this absolute power and going into it, you will know your true self. This true self becomes one with this body and this body then becomes absolute power. Then this body moves, creates and protects everything according to the intention of the absolute power.

When connected with the human form, the absolute power is used in a more meticulous, exquisite and beautiful way. Use this absolute power energy presently and wisely.

In this way, wherever human form and thinking go, absolute power spontaneously goes with them and protects all things from A to Z, very meticulously and thoroughly.

Can you imagine what this is?

351. May 6, 1993. Puchberg, Austria

Present suffering is future success. But if, because of present success, you become complacent, that becomes future suffering. So do not worry about suffering and do not become complacent by success.

Live every day appreciatively and spend every hour and every moment beautifully and stylishly. Then you can experience the taste of suffering and success together, and you will know how to make success and eliminate suffering.

Thus becoming a master of success and suffering, you will know how to eliminate others' suffering and how to make them successful, and you will be able to give others all the benefit and happiness.

Find out what it is to live every hour and every moment beautifully and stylishly.

352. May 7, 1993. Puchberg, Austria.

See yourself.

Put all of your thinking into your body. Your body is the middle point of the whole universe. But if you allow the 84,000 delusions to make you go in 84,000 directions, the universal center point of your body is scattered around, and you forget yourself and your center. And so, from birth to death, many people just wander around and, without doing anything, simply disappear.

Put all of your thinking and mind into your body and see yourself. Right now, how is this body moving? Is it crooked, suffering or in fantasy?

When you realize that you are the center point of the whole universe, what kind of action appears? When you use your body in a crooked way, it makes the whole universe crooked; when you use your body in a comfortable way, it makes the whole universe comfortable.

This small body makes everything move. So research how you should use this body. A clear person uses his form without being hindered by difficulties or happiness, and knows how to enjoy life.

353. May 8, 1993. Puchberg, Austria

Those who know themselves know how to take care of their body and mind. Those who do not know themselves always attach to their body and mind and weaken them. Those who know themselves know how to protect and care for others' bodies and minds. Those who do not know themselves affect others and make their bodies and minds weak.

Find yourself; realize who you are, and protect and care for others and yourself. And while you live in this world, use your body and mind appreciatively. When you leave, go without any feeling.

Something comes from nothing,* and this something exists, depending upon nothing, while that something again goes back to nothing. But while something exists, it always disregards, goes against and disparages this nothing, and thus makes this nothing suffer. But when something realizes this nothing, this something becomes nothing, this nothing becomes something, and nothing becomes nothing.

Here, something refers to 'yu'; nothing refers to 'mu'.

354. May 9, 1993. Paris

Anutara samyak sambodhi means go through the world of ignorance and transcend the world of ignorance. This means realize the level of nothingness which, called *chong gak*, is correct enlightenment.

Go through all the different levels of the human world, reach the nothing world and attain the non-hindered world. At that time, one can eliminate one's devils (delusions, desires, jealousies, anger, lust, fantasies and the intellect) and sit in the Dharma, blow the Dharma flute, hit the Dharma drum, and greet all others who are able to come into this world. With this realization, weak body and mind get soaked with Dharma rain. Then, weak body and mind become healthy, and this body and mind become so light that they can fly in the sky.

Dear Dharma family, I give this hand to you. Take this hand, come into this world, and have a Dharma tango with me.

1 2 3, 4 5

1 2 3, 4 5

355. May 10, 1993. Paris

In the midst of worrying, put your worries down.

In the midst of worrying, do not be afraid of worries.

In the midst of worrying, make worries your friends.

Then, the worries that have become your friends will show you what life is about.

356. May 11, 1993. Paris

Something comes from nothing.

Nothing makes something.

When this something returns to nothing, this something becomes nothing. Then what does this nothing make? Answer this kong-an.

357. May 12, 1993. Paris

Thinking appears. Put it into action. Do not think about it again, and do not even think about thinking. When you can spend the day like this, you can live for a day without hindrance. This is living in the bright life.

One moment of thinking makes two moments of thinking. Those two thoughts then make four thoughts, so you cannot put thinking into action. But even if you do put it into action, six to ten thoughts appear. This is just like living the day in the clouds.

So today, strive to spend the day without thinking.

358. May 13, 1993. Frankfurt

Just because you had a bad dream in the morning, do not feel bad all day long. Until the bad feeling disappears, repeat the mantra.

That dream may have come from karma, from fantasy, or it may be an omen. But bad dreams usually come from delusion. Also, when your body is weak, you can have bad dreams.

Do not attach to bad dreams and when you have them, practice more, eat well, and exercise. But when you have a good dream, spend the day with a good feeling.

Remember, all dreams are created from yourself. So instead of getting caught by dreams, see them. If you had a bad dream, know how to make a good dream. This means your true self can do whatever you want because you are making it.

If you want to have a good dream tomorrow, have a good thought now. If you want to have a good lover's dream, or a make-money dream, or a being-successful dream, have a good thought in this moment.

359. May 14, 1993. Frankfurt

When a difficult situation appears, first relax. If it is difficult to relax, look south, north, east and west and up at the sky. In the sky there are not four directions, but in our human life there are.

The four directions have gates: south gate, north gate, east gate and west gate. When you pass the north gate, there is the south gate; and when you pass the east gate, there is the west gate. When you try to pass all of these gates it is very difficult. So when you pass one gate do not think about the other gates. After you pass one gate, relax.

After you pass all of the gates, break all of the gates and throw them in the ocean; then go without speaking, without hindrance, and relax.

360. May 15, 1993. Frankfurt

Happy mind is happy, sad mind is sad. But while you are practicing you have to endure happy and sad minds. While enduring these minds, it is very difficult, but when you successfully practice enduring them, you can transcend them. When you transcend happy and sad minds, you can see your true self.

But even if you can see your true self, happy mind is happy mind and sad mind is sad mind. Indeed, when you are happy, then you are really happy; and when you are sad, you are really sad. Why is this? Answer this question.

361. May 16, 1993. Paris

You strive to settle your body and mind, but for no reason you feel bad; and even though you do not have a particular sickness, your body is sick and you suffer. During this kind of time, go to a good energy place, and when you are comfortable again, you can return to where you were before. This kind of bodily dysfunction is due to unbalanced nature energy.

When a bird is sick, it knows exactly which direction to fly. When its body is uncomfortable, it flies east or south and returns to its own house. In each of the four seasons, birds find their comfortable place.

362. May 17, 1993. Paris

Small virtue becomes big virtue.
A small offering brings a big benefit.
Giving small happiness to others brings big happiness to yourself.
Small money turns into big money.
Giving small love to others brings big love to yourself.

The small things can change one's life. Remember, this whole universe started from a small, little point. Do not neglect the small things. Every moment, pay attention to the small things. Watch what you are doing and be clear.

363. May 18, 1993. Paris

When somebody states a strong opinion, do not become angry just because it does not fit with your own opinion, do not feel bad about it, and do not get caught by it. In that person's opinion there can be a correct meaning or a crooked meaning, or it can reflect some complex or karma that he or she has.

If that opinion is necessary for you, follow it; and if it is not necessary for you, forget it without saying anything. But if you do not know whether you need it or not, forget about it for a couple of days. The necessary opinion will disappear; the unnecessary one will continue to exist, bother you and make you suffer. At that time, try to forget that suffering mind; that is your practice.

If you can forget everything, at that time you will be able to understand the other person's strong opinion and why he or she had it. Then you can cut off your own opinion and see that it was also ignorant. When you realize this without getting angry and without feeling bad, you can find the correct path together with that person and you will both live harmoniously, with great love.

364. May 19, 1993. Paris

In the sutras it says, "You catch fish with a net, but after you have caught the fish you forget about the net." It is the same thing: you depend upon speech so that you can acquire understanding, but once you understand, you can dispense with speech.

We find ourselves in the silence and, with that true self, we put the truth into action. Then, without making noise, complaints or arguing, this world's countries and families can live beautifully.

Shakyamuni Buddha had six years of silence. In the silence he found himself, but he had to break the silence in order to teach all sentient beings, to teach and lead us to find the truth in 84,000 ways.

But when he went to nirvana, he clearly told us that he had not said anything, and he returned to the silence.

This month is Shakyamuni Buddha's birthday. Try to find his silence.

365. May 20, 1993. Paris

Shakyamuni Buddha found the truth in the silence. His realization was that all sentient beings come from and live in the truth, and that all sentient beings are one family. When he realized this, the three poisons and the 84,000 delusions disappeared.

The three poisons and 84,000 delusions appear from human beings' bodies and minds. So Shakyamuni Buddha used the three poisons to benefit and to protect this one family (all sentient beings), and put the 84,000 delusions to use as teaching methods to deliver 84,000 ways that sentient beings can attain the truth.

This month, we must appreciate and be thankful to this leader of all sentient beings for his great realization, attainment, teachings, love and compassion. Let us be truly thankful to him and put our two hands together in hapchang for him.

Wherever you see a statue of the Buddha, whether large or small, always give him respect just as if you were actually seeing Shakyamuni Buddha. When you see his statue, do not forget to hapchang.

P. S. The three poisons are desire, anger and ignorance.

366. May 21, 1993. Paris

In the seasons, there are spring, summer, fall and winter. In the weather, there are rain, thunder, snow, sun. . . .

It is the same with our situations: we always have many changes; our minds always change. Do not get caught by the changes, and do not make like and dislike. If it is good, enjoy it as it is; if it is bad, accept it as it is. Do not be negative just because it is not what you want.

When you get angry because something does not fit you, this is because your path is not yet deep. So whatever you see, whatever you hear, just see, just hear and pass through. Then you can see the true dharma behind the Buddha's statue.

367. May 22, 1993. Paris

Shakyamuni Buddha found himself after six years of ascetic practice. After he found himself, he was very happy and thought to keep this happiness only for himself and to go into nirvana.

Just then, he realized something important: that he really had not found himself completely, one hundred percent. When he realized that, his happy mind disappeared. Suddenly he felt ashamed of himself and he started practicing again for twenty-one days. That time he found himself one hundred percent, and he realized what was missing.

What he had been missing is so precious it cannot be traded for anything. This treasure is the love and compassion mind which is the true self and is the root of the whole universe. So at that time he made a great vow to himself: "Until all sentient beings in this whole world become emancipated and attain this Buddha place, I will be born and reborn again and again; and while I am helping all sentient beings, I will do so with great love and compassion mind."

Remember, everything comes from great love and compassion mind.

368. May 23, 1993. Paris

Those who want to receive respect and love from others should not talk about others' faults and should not criticize them. Those who judge and complain about the rightness and wrongness of others are especially caught by right and wrong.

Those who talk too much suffer especially in the world of opposites. They do not know what happiness is and at the same time are not happy themselves. Even though a good situation appears, they do not appreciate it and are never happy.

A wise person's soft, beautiful one sentence guides others in the correct way and makes them happy. That person receives respect from others and knows happiness.

Especially in the closest relationships, we should always use respectful language and treat one another with respect. People tend to neglect correct speech and action when they are so close to one another.

369. May 24, 1993. Paris

When one's ego is pleased, one becomes very satisfied.

When one's ego is not pleased, one becomes negative.

Those who have a lot of ego talk too much and at the same time are very negative. They also like to bring others down rather than offering praise.

If you do not want to get caught by all of these things and want to live peacefully, first practice to eliminate your ego. There are four methods: first, do not try triumphing and winning over others; second, do not complain about others; third, strive to learn how to praise others; fourth, strive to learn how to respect others.

When you praise and respect others, that praise and respect energy comes back to you.

370. May 25, 1993. Paris

Those who know themselves and who have really attained independence live with others, and appreciate, respect and help them. These are the truly free people.

Independence is not separation from others. Independence means living in the human world with others and not making them suffer, not bothering them, and only helping them one hundred percent. This is the truly independent and clear person.

Those who want to separate themselves from situations and others, and who want to stay alone in a quiet place, are still caught by situations and others, and are attached to quietude. Such people are very egotistical and are especially caught by the world of opposites and their own selves.

No matter how difficult situations are, do not run away from them; overcome the difficulty. No matter where you go, there will sooner or later be clouds in the sky, and along with them wind and rain.

Before you criticize others, look at yourself.

Before you blame others, look at yourself.

When you can make others happy without speaking, you will be caught by neither independence nor clarity.

371. May 26, 1993. Paris

Because a dragon would like to have a diamond, he practices for hundreds of years. When he earns the diamond, he leaves the world and goes to the sky.

In other words, without the diamond the dragon cannot be free. But if this dragon, who is already in the sky because he has the diamond, becomes attached to the diamond and its value, he cannot be absolutely free. Even though he is in the sky, he will lose the absolute power; he cannot attain absolute freedom and cannot use this power freely.

A wise dragon, even though he loses the diamond, does not attach to it. Instead, he appreciates that he lost it and that, because of the diamond, he had to endure and practice a lot. He really appreciates that.

Through his endurance and practice he attains absolute power and absolute freedom. Then, without existing in the true world he lives in the true world freely, infinitely.

372. May 27, 1993. Paris

Buddha's Birthday Poem

Today is the day Buddha appeared.
The Buddha came into this world, practiced, taught and
    went to nirvana.
From where did he come?

To where did he go?
From where he came, empty.
To where he went, empty.
Also, the practice and teaching places, empty.
Then,
What is the thing which came?
What is the thing which practiced and taught?
What is the thing which went?

When the Buddha was here he only made a net of 84,000 delusions very clearly and then he left. Ignorant human beings got caught by his net of 84,000 delusions, and they are still suffering in it, even today. Pitiful. It makes me very angry.

I have been waiting 365 days for the Buddha to come. Today I heard that he is coming. So I went to the seashore early in the morning with the 84,000-delusions-net and waited for the Buddha to come. He walked towards me with a smile. I put the 84,000-delusions-net over him and threw him into the ocean.

That Buddha disappeared without leaving a trace. Suddenly a lotus flower appeared and floated on top of the ocean and made the whole world bright and shining.

Today the smile of the Buddha in the lotus flower is more bright and content than ever.

Oh dear Buddha, happy birthday on your 2,537 years! Please accept my prostrations and lotus flower lantern, which I offer to you. It is interesting; today the lotus flower lantern shines more than ever.

373. May 28, 1993. Paris

When you practice, try to concentrate on one thing. We have mantra practice, prostration practice, samadhi practice and kong-an practice. Of these, concentrate more on the practice with which you are most comfortable.

In the past, most people found their true self through doing mantra practice. Others found their true self through doing prostrations; others through Samadhi; and still others through the kong-an. You must do all of these practices, but concentrate on that one which is most comfortable for you.

Nowadays, nature energy is very unbalanced. So try to find the practice you can concentrate on one hundred percent so you do not become confused. But regardless of which practice you concentrate on, you must complete your daily mantra assignment. That practice helps to protect you from this unbalanced nature energy.

In my previous experience, I found the truth through doing the mantra, and I attained absolute energy power and absolute power of creation through doing the samadhi.

374. May 29, 1993. Paris

In our original place there is no yin, no yang. In this place there is no name, no form.

When you put Buddha in this original, nothing place, this place becomes Buddha; when you put in God, it becomes God.

Shakyamuni Buddha attained this, so even though he was Buddha himself, he did not call himself a Buddha. He called himself the father and mother of all sentient beings, and addressed his followers and disciples as Buddhas and bodhisattvas. The person whom he called a Buddha became a Buddha; the person whom he called a bodhisattva became a bodhisattva.

Shakyamuni Buddha also took a vow that not until all sentient beings became Buddhas and bodhisattvas would he himself become a Buddha and a bodhisattva.

Dear dharma family, do not attach to name and form. Realize our original place. Become a Buddha and a bodhisattva yourself, and help others to become Buddhas and bodhisattvas themselves.

375. May 30, 1993. Paris

In your daily life, reserve some space. Perform your daily duties diligently, but in your mind always have a reserve of space. Especially when you do not feel well, think about trying to have a reserve of space; and when you are in difficult situations, try to think even more about having a reserve of space. The mind which thinks about wanting to have a reserve of space will release you from suffering and difficulties. That mind is Buddha (true I).

Do not try to find Buddha (true I) outside of yourself. Find Buddha (true I) inside of yourself. Then inside and outside disappear, and you can see that Buddha (true I) which smiles with a reserve of space, which is not lazy, which is without doubt and which works diligently, one hundred percent every day (absolute *Buddhology*).

P. S. Buddhology is the study and practice of the Buddha's teachings and attainment. Reception of the doctorate degree is upon becoming a Buddha yourself.

376. May 31, 1993. Paris

All night long in Buddha.

That time with Buddha was so enjoyable and happy,

That all night long I did not sleep, and then I received the morning.

I am longing for that precious time again.

I received the morning and promised myself again that even during the day I will not get caught by name, form or conditions.

I clearly know that what I see with these eyes and what I hear with these ears is all impermanent, all phantoms. But I get caught by them all of the time and that is why I cannot see Buddha in the daytime.

But in the nighttime I close my eyes, my ears, my mouth and my nose. I forget and put everything down. Then Buddha is in front of me.

NO! I am in Buddha. It is comfortable and happy. Tonight, I am going again into Buddha's embrace and I promise myself that tomorrow morning, even though my eyes and ears open, I will still see Buddha.

377. June 1, 1993. Paris

When you think there are many people who do not like you, it means there are many things which you do not like about yourself. When you think many people like you, it means there are many things which you like about yourself.

Do not get discouraged and disappointed if you think many people do not like you. Instead of getting disappointed, practice and polish yourself until you like yourself. When you practice, the mind which likes yourself and the mind which does not like yourself both disappear and you become comfortable. Then no matter who you deal with, you do not have any fears and you can do your best in your duties.

When you do your best in your duties, success is yours, and then even the person who did not like you before can become a true friend someday. When that person becomes your friend, he or she can be your friend, eternally.

During the time of Shakyamuni Buddha, a person who did not like him became his true disciple and later spread the dharma.

P. S. Also, relax and be happy today.

378. June 2, 1993. Paris

While in the darkness you do not know anything, so you make all kinds of thinking, action and speech. But when the sun shines, that thinking, speech and action show very well.

Then you can see very clearly what you have been doing and at the same time you can see how much you were in ignorance; you feel so ashamed that while in the darkness your thinking, action and speech were so unclear. That is why as one becomes clearer, one feels ashamed and becomes humble.

The shame and humility of one's thinking, action and speech come to shine more, and that radiance makes others bright.

379. June 3, 1993. Schweibenalp, Switzerland

In beautiful thinking, there is a beautiful life. In ugly thinking, there is an ugly life.

Our true mind, which is our original place, is always empty, clean and clear. But thoughts gather like clouds. Negative thinking makes a lot of delusion and suffering. When your thinking is beautiful, however, the clouds turn to sweet rain and make everyone beautiful.

If your thinking is ugly, eliminate it and change it. When you can change your thinking, you can also change your karma. Knowing how to change your thinking, you will know how to eliminate it. When you can eliminate thinking, you can find your true place and you can become a Buddha yourself.

In Buddha's original mind, love and compassion always flow. Wherever this Buddha goes, he makes everyone happy and beautiful.

380. June 4, 1993. Schweibenalp, Switzerland

That mountain in front is high, but how can it be higher than Buddha's mind?

That cloud is floating, but how can it be lighter than Buddha's mind?

That sky is blue, clear and beautiful, but how can it be clearer and more beautiful than Buddha's mind?

It is not only Buddha's mind which is high, light, beautiful and clear. We human beings should not envy and be fascinated by that. How about striving to make your mind high, light, beautiful and clear! That mind which strives and practices is Buddha's mind, and that Buddha is inside of the striving and practice.

381. June 5, 1993. Schweibenalp, Switzerland

Success is when you have someone to whom you can give everything and, even though you give everything, you do not feel that you are missing anything.

The comfortable place is where you can discuss and learn about the truth.

The Buddha path is when you meet someone who leads you to the true path and helps you to open up the wisdom eye.

The person who has these three things is the happiest person in the world. The person who has these three things should not look for something more, and should live without fears and hindrances and should live daily life one hundred percent. Go forward.

382. June 6, 1993. Schweibenalp, Switzerland

A beautiful life does not come from outside and does not come from inside. It comes from one's effort and striving; one makes it directly oneself. That self which makes beauty is the self which brings the beautiful life.

From ugly thinking into beautiful thinking;

From ugly speech into beautiful speech;

From ugly action into beautiful action;

Every moment your self has changes to make.

Look at beautiful nature: the mountains, oceans, forests and fields. Buddha made all of these beautiful things in the Buddha, which means all of these beautiful things are made from our original place. So the clearer we become, the more beautiful we become, because Buddha (truth) means beauty. Ugly means karma.*

Practice to make your mind beautiful. A beautiful mind makes a beautiful radiance come from the body. This shining is for others and makes others happy.
Most karma is ugly, but there is also beautiful bodhisattva karma.

383. June 7, 1993. Schweibenalp, Switzerland
When you try to fulfill your desires, it means that you are still in the karma world. Human desire does not have any end; it always appears continuously. If you try to fulfill it, this only hurts many people and at the same time hurts you, too.

But if you should happen to get into a situation because of your desire, if you know how to use that desire correctly, it will benefit others and will help you transcend the karma world. When you transcend the desire world, you reach the Buddha world. If you want to have desire, have desire for practice and for helping others. Then desire will help you become a hero and a Buddha yourself.

Think of this whole world as one family. If you want to have desire, have the desire to help this one family. This is bodhisattva desire.

384. June 8, Paris
Mahayana and Hinayana Buddhism teach to cut off all attachments and desires which lead to suffering. They want you to cut off everything in order to attain clarity. It is for this reason that they say it is not good to have a lover and is best to remain alone.

But social Buddhism is different. We are not afraid to go into attachment and suffering because through them we attain endurance and transcend attachment and suffering. Then we attain the power to go through difficulties, and our experience is our great teacher and an asset to teach and help others. At the same time, we truly appreciate our partner because if it were not for him or her, how could we experience those attachments and difficulties? Also, we go beyond the difficulties we had in our relationship to enjoy true, infinite love together.

If a wise person has a bad partner, he or she becomes a great philosopher. If a wise person has a good partner, he or she becomes a great bodhisattva.

After you attain true relationship, always converse with one another. This will preserve your true relationship for eternity.

385. June 9, 1993. Barcelona

A long time ago in China, a big-bellied person named Ho Tai wore only rags and carried a large sack on his back. He went from place to place with a smile and he gave good luck to whomever he met because of the connection he had with them through meeting.

Also, a long time ago all the great bodhisattvas adorned themselves with beautiful clothes and jewelry. Whomever they met, whether good or bad people, because of the connection they had with them through meeting, they taught how to have a beautiful mind and body and how to adorn themselves beautifully. The person who received this beauty also attained great love and compassion through it.

These two kinds of people used different forms, but they both taught according to others' levels. Wise people must realize what is beyond form, such as poor and rich, good-looking and bad-looking. They must transcend all of those things and attain the absolute.

When you attain the absolute, you can change your form in many ways. For example, you can sometimes dress in rags and sometimes with beautiful adornments in order to lead all kinds of people to the truth.

386. June 10, 1993. Barcelona

As your path deepens, do not neglect keeping your precepts. When your path deepens, the devils also become stronger; these devils are your own devils. As your path deepens, you may become confused and even think that you are already Buddha.

At such times, you will not want to listen to the master who is leading you on the Buddha- path, and you may neglect your precepts and practice. Should this happen, you must wake up and practice vigorously. When you again practice vigorously, you will know how to appreciate your master and the precepts which keep you on the correct path.

This way, the day when you become a Buddha, you will love your master and the precepts and will also be able to teach others to appreciate their master and to keep the precepts. You will even be capable of loving those who break the precepts and deceive their master, and will practice continuously in order to help them.

This is great love and compassion.

387. June 11, 1993. Ahabah, Spain

While you are traveling the path of truth, which means when you have not yet reached the truth, your body and mind become very sensitive. Many things bother you and you have a lot of suffering.

At this time you must transcend this level through the practice. When you transcend this level, you reach the comfortable level. But at this time you can fall into the non-self level, which is also dangerous because you can attach to the non-self, and you can easily forget the function of your present form.

If this happens, you must practice harder. While depending on the non-self, find the correct function and duty of your present form and mind. When you reach the level of finding your function and duty with this present form, you can finally love yourself, and you will know how to love others and how to receive love.

Buddha's smile is a humble smile, not an egotistical smile.

388. June 12, 1993. Ahabah, Spain

When you are in a difficult or important situation, do not forget to give yourself space. Space makes you relax, so you can balance your own energy and make yourself clear.

Space is not a function of thinking; it is a function of non-thinking, and has no past or future. This space means right now, this moment. Concentrating one hundred percent in this moment is giving yourself space. The Buddha in that space always protects and leads one to the correct path.

Strive to practice seeing that Buddha in the space. When you can see that Buddha in the space, you can transcend difficulty, and you will know what to do in your important situations; and at the same time you will know what absolute relaxation is.

389. June 13, 1993. Ahabah, Spain

Life in karma is selfish life; there one only wants to take care of oneself. Because one is oblivious of others' situations, one speaks, acts and thinks only for oneself. That hurts others, and that suffering returns to oneself.

In life out of karma, you think about others more than about yourself, respect others' opinions and ideas, and care more for others' situations than for your own. You then want to make others more comfortable than yourself. When someone else is happy, you are happy; when someone else feels bad, you feel bad.

Karma life is small I. Life which has transcended karma is big I. Big I is life for others, which is bodhisattva life.

Remember, the karma eye is small like the hole of a needle, but the eye which has transcended karma is bigger than an ocean.

390. June 14, 1993. Ahabah, Spain

For the person who is dry in love, everything is dry.

For the person who is full with love, everything is fulfilled.

When you can love and receive love from one person, that love is full. When you cannot love and receive love from one person, it means that your love is dry. Dry love means that you have a lot of ego and conditions. When you eliminate your ego and conditions, there is always someone waiting whom you can love.

Having ego and conditions means that there is a wall, and that wall keeps things from flowing, making everything dry. Break this wall, give love to others, and receive love from others.

That one love can be ten thousand.

391. June 15, 1993. Paris

A long time ago there was a wise man who owned a gold mine. He had a very sincere employee to whom he entrusted the management of the mine. However, when they transported the gold from one place to another, the owner always watched and went along. The employee felt funny and bad that even though his boss entrusted him with managing the mine, the boss himself always had to be present at the time of transportation.

So one day the employee asked the owner, "Why don't you trust me?" The owner replied, "I do trust you, but you do not trust yourself. That is why I follow you."

This means that you should not complain that others do not trust you. Instead of blaming others, find yourself—who you are, what you are—so that you can trust yourself. When you trust yourself, others will trust you; then there are no doubts or mistrust. That clear mind is not only your mind—it is one with others' minds.

392. June 16, 1993. Paris

Find Buddha (mind, truth). When you realize that you are living in Buddha, this whole universe is yours. Wherever you direct your thinking, it becomes true. Also, without thinking, in the brightness and clarity, happiness flows automatically.

Until you realize Buddha, you overuse your body and it becomes weak. But when you realize Buddha, from that time on your form automatically becomes healthy. The reason is that in clarity you will have the wisdom of how to take care of your body.

Do not be greedy about small things, thus making unnecessary suffering.

Because I cannot share the bright sun and moon with you, I feel anxious. With these ears, hear Buddha's quiet sound; with these eyes, see Buddha very clearly; with these hands, hold Buddha. What more could one wish for?

P. S. For the next week, read this teaching just before you sit samadhi at night.

393. June 17, 1993. Munich

When your body is tired, more delusion appears. At that time, do not only try concentrating to eliminate your delusion. First, relax your body and mind.

The method to relax the mind is to think that there is a Buddha right in front of you and to think that you are living in Buddha. And remember, when spring comes, the flower blooms. Keep that mind so you can eliminate your rushed and restless mind. Have patience, practice and have the mind that until the flower blooms, you will continuously practice.

In practice, that Buddha is always bright and beautiful. The bright and beautiful life of a Buddha is very simple, but at the same time he makes it very rich for others. The bee in the flower always works hard, not for himself but for others, and even today works very diligently.

394. June 18, 1993. Munich

Always look at yourself: your speech, actions and intentions. Every moment, check these things. Success, lack of success, happiness, unhappiness, wealth and poverty are all according to what you do.

The meaning of "in" Buddha is: just like in the mirror. If one's intentions, speech and actions are correct, the mirror reflects the same thing back. And if they are not correct, it also reflects the same thing back.

If you do not act or speak, but you have an ugly intention, that reflects in Buddha and leads to an ugly life. And if you do not know how to act and speak, but your intention is bright and full of love, you become happy and receive a lot of respect from others.

Speech and actions are just like a pen, and intentions are just like ink. Your intention is always reflected in Buddha and is the cause of beautiful or ugly karma.

So first fix and polish your intentions. But if you have beautiful thoughts, actions and intentions, then you become Buddha.

395. June 19, 1993. Munich

In the human world, when you keep the precepts, it is like erecting a high wall which protects you from devils. Within the wall, there is a beautiful garden and castle. There you live in the truth and with true relations. You only discuss the truth and live a truly happy life.

When you do not keep the precepts, life is like wandering in the desert with no sense of direction. In that life, you meet enemies once in a while and live with untrue relations; you are lost and have tremendous suffering.

But in Buddha's world, Buddha deals equally with the person who keeps the precepts and the person who breaks the precepts. Even today, he practices vigorously to make everyone become a Buddha.

I would like to sell the bright, full moon to everybody but I do not yet know the price. That is the reason why I cannot sell it yet. When a person appears who knows and delivers the price, I will sell it to him or her, making a good deal.

396. June 20, 1993. Munich

When you receive the confidence, protection and love of others, do not become unrestrained. The more you receive love, trust and protection from others, continue to be appreciative and humble so your ego does not grow high. Also, when you receive others' trust and love, do not only keep them for yourself. The amount you receive from others, give to others.

Those who realize that they are living in Buddha, and in Buddha's love, know how to give love and how to protect all sentient beings. That is why an awakened person always enjoys life by serving others.

397. June 21, 1993. Paris

As one's path deepens, one becomes brighter and can see oneself very clearly. At that time, more suffering appears because one sees oneself more clearly than one did before: one's faults, ignorance, actions and speech are reflected so clearly, just like in a mirror.

At this kind of time, do not hate or dislike yourself and do not become discouraged. Go on and take another step; practice vigorously so you do not become ashamed of yourself because of what you see in the mirror.

Then, one day what you see in the mirror will be so clear; you will not see any faults, ignorance, action or speech. At that time, happiness will flow like a waterfall.

398. June 22, 1993. Paris

The person who does not trust others is the person who does not trust himself and also the person who has many conditions. Because of such peoples' ignorance, they do not know that they bother others and, because of their doubting minds, even though they meet the true relation and receive true love, they lose that relation and love.

The person who has a lot of doubts does not know what true love is. Because of his doubt, that person never lives comfortably or happily. Doubt is a poison which makes one lonely and leads to having terrible, suffering karma.

Faith is happiness. In faith, what is correct and what is incorrect always clearly appear. In faith, without doubts, everything becomes clear.

The mind which has faith is Buddha mind. That Buddha shatters the darkness, makes other people clear and leads them to the correct path. Faith leads one to good, bodhisattva karma.

Doubt is far away from the truth.

399. June 23, 1993. Paris

Buddha's place is originally bright and clear.

But the *teakkl* fell in there. Where did this *teakkl* come from?

Is it not that Buddha's bright and clear place lost its brightness and clarity because a *teakkl* fell in there?

Over the past 2,500 years, Shakyamuni Buddha and all previous masters practiced very hard and suffered a lot in order to find where the *teakkl* that dirtied Buddha's original bright and clear place came from. How pitiful this is! Some masters went around barefoot for ten or twenty years; some left the lice in their clothes for many years; some never slept for many years and became blind. How terrible, how pitiful!

Dear *teakkl*, because of your presence you make everyone suffer. I will now send you back to your original place where you came from, and I will make everyone comfortable.

In Buddha's comfortable place, the round moon brightly shines and Shakyamuni Buddha and all the masters and *teakkl*s disappear without a trace. Then where did this *teakkl* come from?

Under the bright moon, the sound of repeating the mantra is today and in this moment, clearer and stronger.

Na Mu Kwan Se Um Bo Sal
Na Mu So Ga Mo Ni Bul
Chong Gak Mio Poep Yon Hwa Kyong
Na Mu Kwan Se Um Bo Sal
Na Mu So Ga Mo Ni Bul
Chong Gak Mio Poep Yon Hwa Kyong
Na Mu Kwan Se Um Bo Sal

Na Mu So Ga Mo Ni Bul
Chong Gak Mio Poep Yon Hwa Kyong

P. S. This is an enlightenment teaching. Read it again and again, meditate upon it and attain it.

400. June 24, 1993. Paris

Throw away your greed. Greed is endless. Do not suffer life after life because of greed, which makes bad karma. When you try to fulfill your greed, it does not work and you become angry. Do not make yourself more ignorant because of that anger.

Greed is the cause of ignorance. So cut it off. Greed is just like a cloud. Practice is to eliminate greed.

The bright sky is just like a bodhisattva's face. So make bodhisattva karma in order to make this face smile.

401. June 25, 1993. Bologna

In Buddha's quiet place, without words, I converse with the Buddha and all worries, agonies, tensions and stress disappear. I become one with Buddha.

It is so very comfortable; I will try to relax here a few days. But sorrow arises for the lover I left in my house. So I run home, into that lover's embrace and say, "I am so sorry dear."

At first that lover was confused and made an angry face. But when that lover saw my true, sincere face, the anger disappeared and that lover gave me a beautiful smile and softly embraced me.

Now I clearly realize that paradise is not only in Buddha's world; in the human world, there is a paradise, too.

Thank you very much Buddha and my dear lover!
P. S. What is the true meaning of "that lover"?

402. June 25, 1993. Bologna

Do not make friends with people who do not speak too much but who have a dark face. (This is not referring to skin color but rather to the mind.) You can make friends with people who speak a lot but who have a bright and clear face.

The person who does not talk too much, but who has a clean mind, becomes a bodhisattva. The person who does not talk too much, but who has a lot of greed and jealousy, is brushed off by others.

Always keep your mind clean and do not let it become tainted. Fill your mind for others, to make them happy.

403. June 26, 1993. Bologna

The dharma room: always sweeping and cleaning it.
But dust always appears.
So while sweeping and cleaning, I became exhausted.
I threw the broom away, plopped down on the floor, and cried and huffed.
But the dust piled up more and more.
My exhausted mind and body sat in front of the Buddha.
I repented for everything and asked, "What is my true job?"
Then this sentence appeared, "Without thinking, always polish, always sweep."
This one sentence hit my mind. I was surprised and stood up.
Suddenly, the dust in the dharma room looked so pitiful.

I will clean it up for you.
I picked up the broom which I had thrown away.
1,2,3,4... sweeping and polishing.
If you want to come inside, come as much as you like.
I will clean and polish for you as long as this body exists.

404. June 27, 1993. Bologna

Whatever you do in the dark mirror, it does not appear. Also, whatever thinking appears or disappears does not get caught.

But in the bright and clear mirror, everything can always be seen one by one, very clearly. Whatever thinking appears can easily get caught and can make you suffer more. At that time, do not get caught by thinking. Find the thing which made that thinking and make that thing relax. See that thinking and why it appeared and be careful of your intentions, actions and speech, so you do not make that kind of thinking appear again.

When your intentions, actions and speech are correct, you can find the place of no thinking.

Find that place, and in there only plant a multitude of excellent things.

405. June 28, 1993. Paris

We have a lot of information in our heads. Do not depend only upon that information, judging and deciding things according to it. Find the true I before the world of information, which is no I. Then, from this clear world just look at the information without getting caught by it, and from there judge and decide things and put them into action.

Do not only believe your ears. Trust your bright eye. Buddha's bright eye does not get caught by good or bad; it sees everything correctly, makes everything beautiful, and leads to Buddha's bright and clear place of nothingness.

406. June 29, 1993. Paris

Lately, I am sending very strong energy. Use this energy correctly, and always make your mind comfortable and use it correctly, too.

Do not blame, criticize or judge others. Think of the person who does not like you as your teacher and appreciate the connections which you have with the people whom you know.

With vigorous practice, persevere and relax.

407. June 30, 1993. Paris

Karma body grabs the karma pen and writes one word at a time.

At this time, if the mind is crooked, the words become crooked; if the mind is correct, the writing becomes correct.

But no-mind grabs the no-mind pen and writes.

Whether the words become crooked or correct, they all become beautiful. Then the mountain laughs, the ocean laughs, the moon laughs and the sun laughs.

It makes the whole world laugh hilariously, together.

After laughing hilariously, that place becomes marvelously empty and full of dharma fragrance.

408. July 1, 1993. Paris

When your body is healthy, everyone is healthy.

When your body is sick, everyone is sick.

When your body is comfortable, everyone is comfortable.

Find the master of no-mind and, with that master, make your body healthy and comfortable, all of the time.

The bodies of the Buddhas and bodhisattvas are sick when sentient beings are sick.

The bodies of the Buddhas and bodhisattvas are healthy and comfortable when sentient beings are healthy and comfortable.

When all sentient beings find the master of no-mind, the Buddhas and bodhisattvas will go into nirvana and have an infinite vacation.

409. July 2, 1993. Paris

Once there was someone who lost his direction and was suffering. At that time, he finally met the Buddha and went onto the correct path.

Then someone appeared and said, "That path is not good. It is very rough, so do not continue on it. Instead, go together with me on my path." So this person threw away the Buddha-path and followed the stranger.

While with that stranger, another one appeared and said, "Your path is not good. Come with me." So then he followed that person.

On all of the paths he followed, nothing was clear. So he suffered and was tormented. Then the Buddha suddenly appeared and said, "Do not follow anyone. Until you become a Buddha, only depend upon the dharma, only make friends with the teaching of the dharma, and only have a love relationship with practice. And then the day you become a Buddha yourself, make friends with everyone and go together."

410. July 3, 1993. Paris

Buddha's place is always bright and clear. In it, there is no high or low, ugly or not ugly, good or bad. This place is the place of equality; that is why unexcelled wisdom appears from there.

The path of Buddha is the path of attaining unexcelled wisdom. To go onto this path and become an absolute, free person, first get away from discriminations; do not blame or judge others. Blaming and judging others means that you are blaming and judging yourself.

Always practice and do not be hindered or caught by anything. Get away from the world of opposites, attain unexcelled wisdom and become a complete, correct human being.

411. July 4, 1993. Paris

For those who receive the teachings every day, their path gets deeper and they know what the path of practice is. At the same time, they know what their true self is and discover the true direction of their life.

At this time, one must be careful that one's ego does not grow. When you know yourself, it is easy to get caught by yourself and for your ego to grow. So be careful at this time; always be humble and appreciate others.

Remember, the riper the rice patch becomes, the lower the heads of the rice plants bow down.

412. July 5, 1993. Paris

When you are in a difficult situation, it is easy to practice and find your true self. Through practice, your karma I becomes weaker and you can easily keep your true I.

But when you are in a good situation, it is easy to lose your true I; karma I becomes stronger and your ego grows much bigger. It is just like someone who, being chased by a tiger, climbs up a tree. But while climbing up the tree, drops of honey fall into his or her mouth, and the purpose of going up the tree is forgotten.

As your situation improves, do not neglect your practice. Practice vigorously, become a Buddha yourself, and live life correctly and brightly, in all situations.

P. S. People who live in or who are coming to visit Hawaii should especially pay attention to this teaching.

413. July 6, 1993. Honolulu

Life and our body are impermanent. We do not know when our body will disappear; it is really impermanent.

While this body exists, try not to make the three poisons (desire, anger, ignorance). Through this body, find your true I and only serve others. Only do good things and only make bodhisattva karma so when you disappear, you can do so without regrets and you can come and go again, without hindrance, and have infinite freedom.

414. July 7, 1993. Honolulu

The person who apparently knows what the path is and practices it, but who only thinks his or her opinion is correct and who shows off clandestinely, does not yet really know what the path is, and is not practicing for the path itself but only to make himself or herself more important. This only makes his karma I grow larger.

If you really want your opinion to be important, consider the opinions of others as more important than your own, truly respecting others and their opinions. Then your own opinion will grow in importance and will make everyone happy.

In Buddha's place of equality, there is no you or I. If you show your own I in Buddha's place of equality, it is like placing a rotten log there.

415. July 8, 1993. Honolulu

In Buddha's place there is no sickness or suffering. This place is always in front of us and we always live in it. But because of our sicknesses and suffering, we do not yet see this place of Buddha; we cannot feel it, and we cannot realize that we are living in it.

First, strive to eliminate your mind sicknesses, which are ego, desire and anger; and always direct your body to move and be used to make others happy. Then you can see that Buddha is in front of your eyes, and you can realize and feel that you are living in Buddha.

This Buddha always lives and moves together with you.

416. July 9, 1993. Yun Hwa Dharma Sah

In the mirror, you make the mirror dirty and, as time goes by, you do not even think about cleaning it. You only think about yourself and your body, which makes the mirror dirty. And yet you wish to become a Buddha; this is like trying to make a mirror out of a brick.

Come out from that delusion which dirties the mirror; move and use your body unconditionally, and make others happy. That body which makes others happy can even make a bright mirror out of a brick and can even wash others' dirt and make everyone happy.

417. July 10, 1993. Honolulu

No matter how much correct and beneficial teaching you receive, if you do not follow it, it is useless. It is like trying to give water to a horse that is not thirsty. But a thirsty horse walks to the water himself, drinks, and his thirst is satisfied.

The daily teachings make the thirsty person become a Buddha. But for those who are not thirsty, the daily teachings sound like nothing but nagging and a scolding. Such people always live in the place of sentient beings and do not know when to leave that suffering life; they remain stuck there.

So, are you a thirsty horse or a not-thirsty horse?

418. July 11, 1993. Honolulu

In the world of sentient beings, there are time and space. As the clock ticks, time passes.

As time passed by, the cushion where the Buddha sat 2,537 years ago became old, fell apart and finally disappeared. But that place still exists today. In that place, mountain became ocean and ocean became mountain, many times. Without being hindered by time, that place is always shining and bright.

Do not be sad about or attached to that cushion which became old and disappeared from the place where Buddha sat. The only thing is, do not dirty or defile that place while the cushion exists.

In a way, the cushion which knows Buddha never gets old and never falls apart, even though time passes by. Indeed, as time goes by, it becomes more and more beautiful.

419. July 12, 1993. Honolulu

When there is anger and confrontation, people become blocked, depressed and lonely. At that time, do not lose yourself by attaching to the confrontation. Immediately remind yourself that you are in Buddha and that Buddha is right in front of you.

In Buddha's place, where nothing exists, there can be no anger or confrontation. We are living in this place of Buddha, and so calculating what is right or wrong, good or bad only makes you more ignorant.

Throw everything into the red light of the setting sun over the mountain, and put your lips to the tea cup which is in front of you on the table. Swallow one sip. A rabbit then comes out from the round, full moon and again fills your cup for you.

420. July 13, 1993. Honolulu

Happiness is here.

Do not look far away.

Look here.

Whatever you have now and whatever situation you are in, find happiness there.

You already have everything to be happy.

Do not underestimate yourself.

Digest the fullness, each and everything you already have, one by one.

And be happy.

421. July 14, 1993. Honolulu

When you talk a lot, you easily make many mistakes.

When you talk very little, you easily create many thoughts. If you want to make less mistakes and thoughts:

1. Do not try to show off what you are and how important you are.
2. Do not blame your incapability on ignorance.
3. See everything in a positive way.
4. Transcend what you see through your eyes and what you hear through your ears. See with nothingness and hear with nothingness.

If you do these four things, you will know how to speak appropriately and how to think appropriately.

P. S. What does "See with nothingness and hear with nothingness" mean?

422. July 15, 1993. Honolulu

The blue dragon got the diamond and the white tiger got unexcelled wisdom. Because they rescue and teach all sentient beings, all sentient beings are very happy, and they truly respect the blue dragon and the white tiger.

During the time that the blue dragon practiced to get the diamond and the white tiger practiced to get unexcelled wisdom, they endured many difficulties. Their minds were focused on one single direction and could not be shaken by anything. That is why they got the diamond and unexcelled wisdom, became absolutely free, and attained all the powers by which to make everyone happy.

Your present path of practice is to save yourself and others. While you practice, do not feel bored and never neglect your practice. Even when it seems boring or difficult, always continue on this one direction; keep going until you get your own diamond and unexcelled wisdom.

423. July 16, 1993. Honolulu

Try to understand the person who bothers and hurts you. That understanding mind is Buddha's mind and makes your enemy surrender.

Do not try to escape from the person who makes you suffer; that mind which wants to escape is the mind of sentient beings. Always practice not to get caught by anyone and to attain the place of nothingness.

In the place of nothingness there are no enemies; everyone is one family. If you want to put your mind into something, put it into how to harmonize as one family.

424. July 17, 1993. Honolulu

Do you see?
Do you hear?
The carpet is red, the bird is singing in the garden.

That thing which sees and that thing which hears are so clear. So why does delusion always rise in the minds of sentient beings?

That thing which sees is empty; that thing which hears is empty. If you truly attain this, you can empty out that sentient being mind which gives rise to delusion. In the empty mind, Buddha is sitting there.

The red carpet is beautiful as red and the sound of the bird singing is beautiful as melodic, each just as they are.

425. July 18, 1993. Honolulu

We human beings know how to create style and beauty. Originally we are Buddhas and bodhisattvas. So come out from the karma I as soon as possible, live freely, create beauty, and live a stylish life. This is the correct way of life for human beings.

Remember, our life as human beings is not one of suffering. Look at yourself and your form; see how beautiful you are. Do not taint yourself because of your karma. Live life freely and create as much beauty as you want, as long as you exist in this life and in future lives too.

Go to the bathroom, wash yourself, and give yourself a big smile in the mirror. Handsome? Beautiful? Yes you are!

426. July 19, 1993. Honolulu

Whoever is not clear has a lot of delusion and thinking, and that is why they cannot speak correctly or truthfully. Incorrect and untruthful speech does not earn respect from others and cannot inspire them to listen.

When you speak, speak from the place of no thinking, transcend discriminations, and do not think twice. Even though you do not especially put energy into it, this kind of speech always passes easily into other people's ears and does not irritate those who listen to you.

No matter how formally beautiful some speech is, if it comes from a lot of thinking—I, my, me and discriminations--it will always irritates others' ears and make you very lonely and isolated.

427. July 20, 1993. Honolulu

In front of karma I's eyes, Buddha is also karma I.

In front of Buddha's eyes, karma I is a Buddha.

Buddha is not afraid to appear in front of karma I. But karma I is afraid to appear in front of Buddha. So karma I always speaks poorly and complainingly about Buddha, and tries to bring Buddha down to its own level. When it does this, karma I becomes very happy.

But no matter what kind of disparagement and complaint Buddha receives, Buddha never blames karma I. Even if Buddha gets hurt, Buddha always wants to lead karma I to the correct way.

Always practice and strive to turn karma I into a Buddha. Buddha took a great vow that Buddha will not go into nirvana until every karma I is turned into a Buddha.

428. July 21, 1993. Honolulu

When you do not know what you really want, do not become depressed and do not try to figure out what you really want. Bury everything in the exquisite dharma and do not give rise to thinking. Bury everything there.

In the exquisite dharma, create yourself and lead yourself to the correct way. The exquisite dharma will show and teach you what you really want and will help you to attain it.

Remember, what you are doing right now is in fact precisely what you wanted to do. Do not forget that.

429. July 22, 1993. Honolulu

Mind and body sicknesses come from karma. When you eliminate your karma, your mind and body sicknesses disappear, and, at the same time, that mind and body which came from karma also disappear.

But this mind is here and this body is here. So after you eliminate your karma, this mind is whose mind and this body is whose body? And where did the mind and body go which disappeared?

430. July 23, 1993. Honolulu

Fix your own problems, sicknesses and blockages before you interfere in the lives of others. If you really want to help others, wait until they ask you for your help, and while you are waiting, hope that they are doing well.

The mind which, without jealousy, wishes that others are doing well is the mind which leads one to the correct path of fixing one's own problems, sicknesses and blockages.

Saving all sentient beings means saving oneself. Others' happiness is my happiness; others' sadness is my sadness. We are never separate.

431. July 24, 1993. Honolulu

Because of the past, recollections of the past, delusions in the past and desires for the future, the present, right now, is not clear. But recollecting the past renders the present more unclear than does thinking about the future. Normal people can begin to remember the past when they are three years old; some begin earlier, at only two years old.

Do not get hung up by recollecting the past. Recalling the past is wasting your time in the present and makes the present unclear.

Especially avoid or cut off recollections which are negative. Yesterday, one hour ago, one minute ago—all that is past. Forget all negativities and in this present moment only think about the bright future. The moment of thinking about a bright future is a bright, present moment.

When you practice like this, you can be happy and you can have a bright present and future. At the same time, it will transform the ugly past, making it bright, enabling you to appreciate what was bad and ugly in the past and to live everyday clearly, without any hindrance.

432. July 25, 1993. Honolulu

Even though practice people's bodies become old, their minds become younger. They become younger and younger, and return to being a child. For example, one's body may be eighty years old but one's mind is like a three-year-old's.

But if one does not practice, one's body may be fit like a three-year-old's, but one's mind will be like that of an eighty-year-old. Can you imagine how heavy and how much suffering that is?

Is your mind right now eighty years old or is it three years old? If you say it is eighty years old, that is not correct; and if you say it is three years old, that is also not correct. Then what is it?

Tonight in the fish pond at the Hilton Hawaiian Village in Hawaii, the three lotus flowers floating on top of the eighty carps are more beautiful and shiny.

433. July 26, 1993. Honolulu

When someone does bad action and disappoints you, point it out to him or her and then do not speak about it anymore. Wait. And while you wait, do not hold and keep what that person did; forget about it.

This is the way to make others realize what they are really doing and show them the correct path. At the same time, you do not get caught by their actions. When you do not get caught by the disappointing actions of others, it helps make you bright and clear.

434. July 27, 1993. Honolulu

When you receive teachings, appreciate them. Through them you learn what you did not know before; and even though you may sometimes re-learn something which you knew before, appreciate it.

Do not be like a monkey or parakeet with the teachings. Take one more step and, through that teaching, cut off your desire and wanting mind, become a Buddha, and do for others what they want.

Do bodhisattva action without any I. This is true I's desire and wanting mind.

435. July 28, 1993. Honolulu

The shine of the light in the place of nothing eliminates delusions and devils and always cleans this place.

When returning to the place of nothing, one always feels lonely; this is because one must cut off one's desire and wanting mind.

But when you achieve loneliness one hundred percent, you can attain the place of nothing, and in that place, the light shines and its radiance saves all beings, both living and dead.

436. July 29, 1993. Honolulu

Eliminate your own darkness, give brightness to others, and at the same time, eliminate the darkness which is coming from others. Make everyone bright.

Your own darkness transmits darkness to others and, at the same time, receives the darkness which is coming from them, thus making you suffer more in even deeper darkness.

437. July 30, 1993. Honolulu

Put everything (desires and wanting mind) into the O and take a bath there. See what you were before you went into the O: were your desires and wanting mind correct or incorrect? Were you making others suffer because of them?

When you truly put yourself into the O, you feel sorry because of the suffering your desire and wanting mind caused others. At that time, also put your sorrow into the O. Then your true I, which is in the O and is without desire, wanting mind or thinking, can do one hundred percent whatever the situation you are in requires. Then you will appreciate your present situations and positions, and you will thoroughly realize that your true job is only to make others happy.

Doing so, you can realize that, while before going into the O, your desire and wanting mind was so big and greedy, now they are nothing but phantoms and dew drops. When you realize this, you will automatically take the vow that from then on you will live your life without any desire or wanting mind.

438. July 31, 1993. Honolulu

Always think beautifully.

As time goes by, the body becomes old and uncomfortable, just like an old car which starts breaking down. But do not think about what is breaking down. First, fix your thinking. Always consider how to make beautiful thinking.

Even when someone makes a mistake, think about how to forgive that person; think about how to make others comfortable, without bothering them. For example, even if a situation is ugly, try to think in a beautiful way.

439. August 1, 1993. Yun Hwa Dharma Sah

If when dealing with others you control your karma I, they will appreciate and love you, and will receive your love.

But when you cannot control your karma I, no matter how much effort you make to do things for others, they will not accept you. At the same time, your efforts to help them will bother them and they will doubt your love.

440. August 2, 1993. Yun Hwa Dharma Sah

The Yun Hwa Dharma Sah Buddha and great bodhisattvas are so beautiful and have such august countenances. This Buddha and these bodhisattvas have unexcelled wisdom and great supernatural penetration power. They want to save all sentient beings; that is why they are sitting here in Yun Hwa Dharma Sah.

Great Buddha and bodhisattvas, please save many, many sentient beings and bring them to the path to become great Buddhas and bodhisattvas, making this land a beautifully adorned Buddha land. Please protect all beings every day, every moment.

Also, Medicine King Buddha, who especially has absolute power and wants to heal the illnesses of all sentient beings, please heal all human beings' bodies and enable them always to be healthy.

Thank you very much for coming here, all Buddhas and bodhisattvas.

P. S. Yun Hwa Dharma Sah has special healing energy, and that is why the Medicine King Buddha is here. People who have body sicknesses should especially come here to receive this energy and to heal their bodies. This Buddha will especially help people during this kind of time when the nature energy is so unbalanced.

441. August 3, 1993. Yun Hwa Dharma Sah

The I which has no-I has no place for the ego.

In the I which has I, ego becomes the boss. This ego I cannot see or think about the no-I; it can only imagine, through fantasy, that it sees the no-I.

The ego is always born and appears in the world and creates suffering during the times of birth, life and death.

When you eliminate ego, I disappears. Then where is I? And where is the I which has no ego?

The smiles of the Yun Hwa Dharma Sah Buddhas are very profound and beautiful.

442. August 4, 1993. Yun Hwa Dharma Sah

The place of I: wisdom is only one second.

The place of no-I: wisdom is twenty-four hours.

The wisdom which is in twenty-four hours is not mine and is not especially for specific others; it is for everybody, and it makes everyone comfortable, helping them live life freely and happily. This wisdom, which is without hindrances or blockages, creates everything.

Find no-I and let wisdom-light shine incalculably; create an appreciative, thankful life and make everyone happy.

What is this wisdom light? Oh beautiful you, please be happy.

That bright light beyond the beautiful face is shining. But how can I share it with you? Shall I sell it for one cent or for twenty-four cents? Tell me how much should I sell it for.

443. August 5, 1993. Yun Hwa Dharma Sah

As practice deepens, you become just like a mirror. Whoever you meet, your speech and action change according to that person's karma and personality.

In that moment of change, do not blame yourself for changing; perceive how you change, take it as your learning material, and use it to help others turn their negativity into positivity. Help lead them onto the path of finding the place of no change.

The path to the place of no change is the path to true I. Lead others onto this path, and practice yourself in order not to become dirty or hindered by others, just like a lotus flower.

444. August 6, 1993. Yun Hwa Dharma Sah

Practice people, do not be nosy or try to find things out about others. Only strive to find yourself. When you know who you are, you will automatically know who others are.

When you truly find yourself, your complaints about others will disappear and you will realize that others' mistakes are your own mistakes. When you attain that, you will strive to fix yourself and will always polish yourself, just as if polishing a mirror.

445. August 7, 1993. Honolulu

While we are living, there are many things to do. If those duties are only for oneself, they make more suffering. But if those duties are for others and are to make others happy, then, no matter how difficult they are, one can accomplish them without suffering.

Coming into this world and helping others is everyone's function. No matter how difficult it is, sacrificing oneself for the big purpose is a beautiful thing.

446. August 8, 1993. Honolulu

When you are in a difficult situation, it is hard to conquer the difficulty. But while in difficulty, just as in darkness, there is always a hint of light. No matter how difficult the situation may be, if, while in the difficulty, you strive to find that hint of light, your effort will always lead to the discovery of the light's source.

So when you are in difficulty, do not get caught; do not attach to your difficulty and do not drown in it. Always strive and practice to conquer it. The person who does so will always succeed.

447. August 9, 1993. Yun Hwa Dharma Sah

No matter how much heavy karma you may have and how bad your personality may be, in the face of true love that karma disappears and that personality becomes good. It is just like when dark clouds disappear in the sunshine.

When you meet someone who has heavy karma and a bad personality, do not blame him or her for this. Appreciate the connection which you have with one another; meeting someone is always due to the karmic connection you share.

Practice to eliminate your karma and fix your personality so you will be able to love others unconditionally. Practice also to harmonize with others so you can receive and give true love.

448. August 10, 1993. Yun Hwa Dharma Sah

If when you see one, you attach to one, you lose one and you also lose ten.

When you can see that there are not one or ten, then you can earn one, you can earn ten; you will know how to use one, how to use ten, how to care for one, and how to care for ten.

One is important as one, and ten is important as ten. Each has its correct duty and function.

$$1 + 10 = 11$$

449. August 11, 1993. Yun Hwa Dharma Sah

As your path gets deeper, what you have done in the past and your thoughts about it appear more clearly, and you come to know why you have your present situation. Just be happy that you know these things clearly, and do not get caught by those past situations which were negative and do not feel sorry because of them.

Open more fully that bright aspect of yourself which knows all of these things and practice to keep it. That bright aspect is Buddha and is the true I, and that true I is your master. That bright master made the universe and controls nature.

The person who knows the true I does not have any fears and lives life correctly, every day.

450. August 12, 1993. Yun Hwa Dharma Sah

When you escape from a difficult situation, that difficult situation comes back again.

When you overcome a difficult situation, that difficult situation does not come back again.

When you want to overcome a difficult situation, do not cut others off. First, cut off yourself, bow your head, and bow your mind too. Then, just like a tree that flexibly bows over and cannot be broken by even the strongest wind, you can withstand and overcome any difficulty.

After you overcome a difficult situation, continue practicing to become even humbler. Forget about the difficult situation you had and forget about what you wanted. When you do this, as time goes by you can get everything you wanted.

451. August 13, 1993. At the Volcano Ceremony

Dear Fire Goddess:

We sentient beings are becoming comfortable. We sentient beings are cutting off the three poisons and are harmonizing for the benefit of each other. We sentient beings are coming out of our I-my-me, are cutting off all of our jealousies and competitiveness, are becoming truly happy for others' success and happiness, and are striving for others to become more successful. We sentient beings are practicing vigorously in order to go into Buddha's absolute world. We sentient beings, one by one, are becoming Buddhas and bodhisattvas.

Dear Fire Goddess:

Please cut off all the worries and agonies you have because of us sentient beings. From now on, in this moment, please be relaxed, tranquil and still in Buddha's place of nothing. Thank you very much.

Na Mu Kwan Se Um Bo Sal

Na Mu So Ga Mo Ni Bul

Chong Gak Mio Poep Yun Hwa Kyong

P. S. This is a very important teaching, especially for practicing people. Through this teaching practicing people will understand more what Ji Kwang Dae Poep Sa Nim's intention and purpose are in teaching her students.

452. August 14, 1993. Yun Hwa Dharma Sah

Those who get upset due to not getting what they want, those who get upset because others do not listen to them, those who talk too much, always insisting that they are right and irritating others, do not know what happiness is. Such people, even though happiness appears, reject it; they become upset and disappointed, and complain that they are not happy.

Practice person: always look into yourself just as if you were looking into a mirror; always practice in order to polish yourself, to not irritate others, and to not disappoint them. Those who know how to make others comfortable know true happiness, and happiness will never leave them.

453. August 15, 1993. Yun Hwa Dharma Sah

There is nothing more interesting than fixing your own personality. As your personality changes, so does your life.

Change a square personality into a round personality; change a poking personality into a smooth personality; change an angry personality into a soft personality; change a show-off personality into a humble personality; change a smart-aleck personality into a tranquil personality; change a doubting personality into a trusting personality; and change a melancholy personality into a bright personality.

While you are fixing your personality in this way, you can see very clearly how you change; and seeing those changes is very interesting and a lot of fun. You will become a profound and truthful person, and this is the path to liking yourself. Through liking yourself in this way, you learn how to love others, and in doing so will be infinitely happy, without any I.

454. August 16, 1993. Yun Hwa Dharma Sah

Do not look at others according to your own thinking. Before you look at others, look at your thinking. If in that thinking there is no other or I, then you can see others.

The heads of those who see others is always full of thinking about how to help others, how to lead them to the correct path, and how to make them comfortable and happy.

For the person who only sees himself, the sky is full of dark clouds, thunder and storms. For the person who sees others, the sky is full of white clouds that lightly shower the earth, gently quenching people's thirst.

Do not be the tail of a snake. Be the head of a dragon.

455. August 17, 1993. Yun Hwa Dharma Sah

Wherever absolute energy goes, the Buddhas and bodhisattvas become comfortable, all nature becomes comfortable, and all sentient beings become comfortable. Especially in places where this absolute energy settles, angry nature's anger disappears and nature becomes relaxed and comfortable.

The practice person who has this connection with absolute energy should not worry. Just relax, practice regularly, and do your daily work one hundred percent.

[*Note: On August 15, 1993, a hurricane was expected to hit Hilo, Hawaii. The island was in a state of alert and many people did not go to work, as they were preparing for the arrival of the hurricane. Dae Poep Sa Nim told us that the hurricane wanted to come and that she had to do something to stop it. First she said that it would come but that she would try to minimize its consequences. Some hours later, Dae Poep Sa Nim told us that she was negotiating with it. Finally, she told us not to worry at all about the hurricane and to concentrate on our practice.*

Never before in Hilo have we seen two days and two nights so clear and without any rain as we did those two days during which the hurricane was expected. All of Dae Poep Sa Nim's students who were at the Lotus Flowers Farmhouse in Hilo are witnesses of this event and thank Dae Poep Sa Nim, Buddha and nature's energy for stopping this disaster.]

456. August 18, 1993. Yun Hwa Dharma Sah

In the place of nothing, a bright light appears. In that bright light, everything becomes relaxed and comfortable. To you who receive this bright light, it brings paradise.

You are practicing in order to come into this bright light.
You are practicing in order to always stay in this bright light.
You are practicing in order to keep this bright light.
You are practicing in order to become a bright light yourself.
You are practicing in order to give this bright light to everyone.
Then what is this bright light?

The round, bright light in front of the mountain shines on your round face. In its two round eyes are the Buddhas and bodhisattvas. Together they hapchang, together they have appreciation, and together they wish for comfort. With their hands held in hapchang, they together offer and receive this flower of bright light.

The number of these flowers of bright light is multiplying:

1, 2, 3, 4, 5....

457. August 19, 1993. Yun Hwa Dharma Sah

Everyone: please become more and more comfortable. Think about Buddha's realm which has no agonies or worries and be comfortable.

This saha world is the realm of action. According to actions made, agonies and suffering appear. But when actions are done, return again to the place of nothing and become comfortable.

While you are in action, do not only attach to your actions. Each day, go often into the realm of Buddha through the mantra, be comfortable and tranquil, and return to the realm of action to act without being caught by any hindrances or attachments. When nighttime comes, put everything down and comfortably go to bed for the next day's bright action.

458. August 20, 1993. Yun Hwa Dharma Sah

Through the connections you had in your last life, in this life you come to have the family and friends that you do. But even with family and friends, when the connections with them are finished, you separate.

The connections that you make through the dharma always remain, infinitely. Even though you may separate for a while because of your duties and situations, you come back together again and these relationships become deeper and deeper.

All of you who are connected through the dharma, please be happy and comfortable and make all of your wishes come true, under Buddha's protection.

459. August 21, 1993. Yun Hwa Dharma Sah

It is difficult for people who have a lot of doubts to succeed in life. Even if they have an opportunity to succeed, they tend to lose the chance. Even if they meet a truthful person (such as a master or a good friend), due to their doubts it is difficult for them to keep that relationship, and they become lonely again.

Doubtful peoples' energy always makes others uncomfortable, and so it is difficult for others to respect them. Also, if someone gives them a job, because they are doubtful, they do not want to do it one hundred percent and they do not do it sincerely. Because of this, others cannot rely on or trust them.

Doubtful people have a lot of jealousy, and even if someone wants to give them the truth, the truth is blocked by it. Doubtful people also have a lot of thinking, and thereby don't give a clean impression to others, appearing instead as untrustworthy people.

If you think you have a lot of doubt, try changing yourself into a trustful person. As you become trustful, your whole life changes; you are led to the bright path, and happiness like you never expected comes.

When things do not work out the way you had expected and hoped they would, do not blame others. At that time, see yourself and see how your doubts made things not work out as you had hoped they would.

460. August 22, 1993. Yun Hwa Dharma Sah

Eliminate ego.

Eliminate anger.

Eliminate jealousy.

Eliminate your own karma which makes all of this.

Eliminate yourself.

When you can do this, you can become the humblest and kindest bodhisattva, living always in the bright light, happily, and creating beauty. Through this creativity, you will receive love from all others and will be able to live life appreciatively, moment-to-moment, infinitely.

461. August 23, 1993. Honolulu

Do you see this Buddha's absolute world?

Do you see this Buddha's bright and clear place?

If you put a flower in it, this place becomes a beautiful flower.

If you make a smiling face in it, this place becomes smiling.

If you become sad in it because you are getting old, fat and ugly, this place becomes old, fat and ugly.

But, even though you have a wrinkled face, if you smile in this place, and if you think of your fat as a sign of richness and decide that for the rest of your life you want to make others happy, that decision makes you become a bodhisattva.

And if in this place you continuously do bodhisattva action, you become a bright and clear Buddha. That Buddha's radiance will never suffer because of birth, old age, sickness or death. This radiance will shine continuously throughout the whole world and, because of it, all nature and sentient beings will shine together.

In the non-dark world, everyone be happy and only make beauty.

The lotus flower in the dirty mud disappears without a trace and its fragrance fills the whole universe.

462. August 24, 1993. Honolulu

Today is Seven Gods Day. These gods take care of people's health and help make their wishes come true.

Today, I made a benediction that all practitioners may practice vigorously and become Buddhas, that all practitioners will be healthy until all sentient beings are saved, that your wishes may come true, and that you may live a long life.

Today, I also made a special benediction for all of our Lotus Sangha and for all who have the energy line.

463. August 25, 1993. Honolulu

A practice person should doubt about himself once in a while.

When you think that you can really trust yourself, that means your Ego is becoming bigger. When you think that you cannot trust yourself, then you suffer.

Doubting about yourself once in a while means that you are looking into yourself. By doubting about yourself, you are organizing yourself.

If while you are organizing yourself there are no doubts and no overconfidence, then your true I will live correctly without suffering.

464. August 26, 1993. Honolulu

When going into the beehive, you wear special protective clothing so that you don't get stung by the bees. Social life is just like going into the beehive. But no matter how much protective clothing you wear, if there is even a tiny hole inside, you will get stung.

Those who know about bees, who know how to become one with them, and who know how to become their friend, are those who can go into the beehive without protective clothing and stay there without getting hurt.

Being a practice person means going into the beehive without protective clothing and becoming one with the bees, becoming their friend. This is why you are practicing. Afterwards, you will know how to teach the bees so they do not hurt others.

465. August 27, 1993. Honolulu

Today, try to put all of your thinking down. When thinking appears:
1. Only think about good things
2. Only think about how to make others (your teacher, master, wife, husband, friends and family) happy.
3. Practice to go into the place of no thinking.
4. Only think about going into the place of no thinking.
5. Relax completely and put everything down.

466. August 28, 1993. Honolulu

In human beings' relationships, the nicer you are to others, the bigger their expectations become. Consequently, when you are not nice to them, they complain because they feel you are not taking enough care of them. Also, if you benefit them ten times, but one time you do not, because of that one time they complain. The other ten times do not count; they only complain about the single time you did not benefit them.

So when you have a relationship with somebody, do not overdo it; and also do not do less than is necessary. Always try going the middle way. Going the middle way means you do not expect or complain about anything.

Strive to empty your mind of expectations and complaints. Then you can have smooth relationships all of the time.

467. August 29, 1993. Honolulu

Those who are greedy have a lot of expectations. They always want to receive care and special treatment from others, and always want someone to notice them.

Those who are not greedy do not have expectations. When someone cares for and treats them well, they always appreciate it and strive to repay more than what they receive. If someone notices them, they feel ashamed.

When the sun shines, the lotus flower shines more brightly; the rose, with its many thorns, shrivels.

468. August 30, 1993. Honolulu

The human mind is built in such a way that even if one does nothing, the mind still automatically thinks about darkness and fears. Practicing is transforming your dark and fearful thinking into brightness and fearlessness. If we do not practice, we continue suffering in darkness and fear; we will continually be born and live therein.

Always strive to change darkness into brightness and fears into fearlessness. This striving is like a tree in a dark forest that grows out of the thick shade into the sunshine and sways there freely.

P. S. From the year 1990 to 2000, the mind's tendency to go into darkness and fear is much stronger. This is because of nature's energy and not individuals' minds. Nature's energy is getting darker and more negative than before. More and more people are going into darkness and fears. People's true mind is becoming obscured and they are losing their confidence.

469. August 31, 1993. Honolulu

True I comes from Buddha's world. True I becomes Buddha and protects Buddha's world. True I wants to make Buddha's world beautiful. That is why true I leads to the path of Buddha: to make everyone become a Buddha.

This true I that comes from Buddha's world is connected to nature and cannot be separated from it. Because of that connection, true I exists and acts.

When true I appreciates, protects and makes nature beautiful, true I is doing its correct function. Then nature also follows true I's intention, protecting and caring for the true I. So true I also leads nature to the path of Buddha and helps it to become a Buddha. That world in which everyone has become a Buddha already shines throughout the universe.

Please practice to find this true I.

470. September 1, 1993. Honolulu

The reason why we have to have a good mind and do good actions is because the true I is in the place of good. The place of bad does not have true I. In the place of no true I, there is always suffering and insecurity. But when your speech, action and thinking are in the place of good, you become one with your true I, you feel secure and confident, and that makes you become clear. That is why there is no suffering in the place of good.

Good actions do not have hindrances or blockages. The place of no hindrances and no blockages is the world of brightness, which is Buddha's world. Good (or good nature) is the law of the universe. In good nature there is bright wisdom and great supernatural penetration power.

Your good actions give you great freedom.

Please be a good boy or a good girl.

471. September 2, 1993. Honolulu

Always watch your mind.

The human mind is very delicate. When you see darkness, the mind becomes dark; when you see brightness, the mind becomes bright.

For example, when you see a negative movie, the mind becomes very negative; when you see a good or positive movie, the mind becomes positive.

Wherever you go and whatever you do, try to get away from negativity and seek brightness. But when your mind is completely empty and always as bright and clear as a mirror, whether you encounter negativity or positivity you do not get caught by them. You can just see negativity and positivity as what they are and know how to enjoy every moment.

472. September 3, 1993. Honolulu

Do not complain if somebody else is not like you.
Do not be happy if somebody else is like you.
In the forest there are many different kinds of plants and trees. These plants and trees seem to be similar but each one of them is different.

It is the same with human beings. In this world there are six billion people and all of them seem to have similar personalities but everyone is different. This is the world of form.

Practice to attain the absolute, clear world beyond the world of form. When you attain it, neither similarity nor difference hinders you. You will know how to see clearly, how to understand correctly, and how to love each one of them. Then you can live a comfortable life, infinitely.

473. September 4, 1993. Honolulu

There are two different countenances.

Buddha's world is clear and bright: therein is a smiling countenance. The world of form (sentient beings' world) is crowded with wanting, hindrances and attachments: therein is a sad countenance.

Whoever realizes one hundred percent the smiling countenance will know Buddha's world, what Buddha is, and through his own smile will become a Buddha.

474. September 5, 1993. Honolulu

In the mind of gratitude there is no ego.

When you thank others and when you receive thanks from others, you become one with them and there is no me or you; everybody is equal. In gratitude, there is no anger or jealousy and all conflicts disappear; then we can have truthful relationships with others. At that time, you can rescue yourself from the social spider web. You will know who you are, you will know how to keep yourself clearly without dirtying yourself, and you can live comfortably, without any worries.

Be grateful to people you do not like as well as to those whom you do like. Why do we have to be grateful to people we do not like? If you realize why you have to be grateful to people you do not like, no matter who you are with, no matter who you meet, you will live comfortably without hindrances.

At this very moment repeat 108 times: "Thank you very much, everybody."

P. S. I have a close family friend who is going to celebrate her 108th birthday this year. This person's long-life secret is that she eats any kind of food available, she sleeps very well, and she is grateful to everyone and for everything.

475. September 6, 1993. Yun Hwa Dharma Sah

The person who always verifies what is right and what is wrong and tries to do everything perfectly creates suffering for both himself and others.

A wise person does not verify what is right and what is wrong. Whatever job is given, he or she goes into action without thinking and questioning. As time goes by, everything works out correctly for this kind of person, whom everyone will follow and respect.

476. September 7, 1993. Yun Hwa Dharma Sah

As the path gets deeper one does not get trapped in the past and does not have expectations about the future: one only appreciates the existence of this moment, in this world, today.

In the course of each day, one strives not to make others suffer and avoids troubling nature, acting modestly and not showing off to others.

The sun's brightness comes from inside.

In Buddha's world one speaks but does not speak, sees but does not see, and hears but does not hear.

477. September 8, 1993. Yun Hwa Dharma Sah

The closer the relationship you have with someone, the more you must give respect. When you become too familiar, you can easily create conflict, lose respect for and disparage each other.

Children should always respect their parents; parents should always respect their children; a husband should always respect his wife; a wife should always respect her husband; and close friends should always respect one another.

When you receive respect from each other, you can do your duties correctly and will be able to bring out your individual talents, creating an appreciative and beautiful life.

Those who want to control others will never receive respect from them. Respecting others means respecting oneself.

Today, repeat 300 times: "I will respect others."

478. September 9, 1993. Yun Hwa Dharma Sah

Live without worries. Worrying makes mind and body suffer and causes the biggest sicknesses.

In times of worry, your highest thought should be about Buddha and your lowest thought should be about doing your duty one hundred percent.

In times of worry, always think about how to help others more effectively, and before that thinking disappears, move your body and put that thinking into action.

479. September 10, 1993. Yun Hwa Dharma Sah

Those who lack faith in themselves always want to show off and check others. Being so recalcitrant, they cause others suffering.

Those who have faith in themselves do not show off and always respect others' opinions, helping them and offering them service. This is just like a shepherd who does not check what the individual sheep are doing but always gives them freedom, making them comfortable and leading them along the correct path.

People who have faith in themselves speak with smiles. But people who do not have faith in themselves speak with their tongues.

480. September 11, 1993. Yun Hwa Dharma Sah

The sun and the moon are above the clouds, always doing their duty sincerely, without expecting anything, and making everyone happy.

If you do your own duty sincerely, without expecting anything, success will always follow; you will become a needed person and will always live an appreciative life.

An expecting mind creates ego and jealousies.

481. September 12, 1993. Honolulu

No matter what situation there is, there are always blockages and hindrances. Even if your purpose and goal are clear, while you are pursuing them there are always hindrances. At such times it is easy to doubt yourself. And when you cannot break your hindrances and blockages, you may stop moving along your path, and this causes suffering and waste.

Whoever conquers their hindrances and blockages is successful. Whoever cannot conquer their hindrances and blockages always fails, no matter what he or she does.

For example, when you dig a well, dig only one hole. While you are digging, just because there is a big rock, do not give up; put all of your energy and life into eliminating that rock. Then, behind the rock you will find delicious water waiting for you.

Smart and intelligent people hurt themselves and others. Ignorant people hurt others. But wise people always give benefit to themselves and to others.

P. S. During the past year, I made a daily teaching every single day. While giving out these teachings, some people understand, digest and appreciate them; but some people do not understand, do not know how to digest them, and many times they do not agree with the teaching. When I see a person who does not digest and does not like the teaching, I get hurt, but this is okay. The reason these kind of people do not like the teaching is because they think they know the teaching already and feel that the teaching is not great for them, and this makes their egos grow higher.

If there is no teaching, how would you be able to see yourself and judge how much you know? These daily teachings are for the person who knows everything, for the one who does not know, and for the one willing to learn. They are for everybody.

Those who know the teachings: do not disparage them. Those who do not understand the teachings too much: do not be discouraged. I want you to just read the teaching every day, seeing yourself and the meaning beyond that.

P. P. S. Why am I putting the above P. S. in this teaching? Think about it.

482. September 13, 1993. Honolulu

No matter where you go, no matter what kind of situations you are in, do not forget your position, duties and functions.

The human mind easily changes according to the situation and the people present, thus making you forget your position, duties and functions. Furthermore, you may even forget your vows and goals and quit halfway, thus going into deep suffering.

This is just like people who want to get enlightened, and so go to the mountains to practice. But there they indulge in the beautiful scenery and the peacefulness of the mountains, forgetting why they went there.

So always see what your position, duties and functions are.

483. September 14, 1993. Honolulu

For a diamond to become shining, bright and clear, it must first be cut correctly and polished.

For you to receive respect from others and to be better, more important, and have a higher position than others, you must cut and polish yourself.

Cutting and polishing yourself is not easy. But while you are doing so, your I disappears. Then, even if you do not want to receive respect from, be more important than, or have a higher position than others, you will get everything as time goes by.

484. September 15, 1993. Honolulu

When actors or actresses act, if they think about their I, they cannot perform the roles given to them. They will receive complaints from others and will lose the position of being an actor or actress.

If you think about your I while doing your proper duties and functions, you cannot perform them correctly and cannot keep your position. In addition, others will not trust or respect you. You will finally become an unreliable person, get lost, and have difficulty having good opportunities again.

So, if according to your position you do your duties and functions correctly, one hundred percent, you can transcend your conditional small I. You can find the unconditional true I, keep your position, and do your duties and functions correctly.

485. September 16, 1993. Honolulu

Believing is good. Believing means that you are able to believe in and trust yourself. If you can believe in and trust yourself, no matter what kind of disappointment appears, your belief can overcome it and deepen trust in yourself. Such believing can even chase away devils and lead you to become a Buddha.

Not believing is like a bowl full of water with a crack, through which the water leaks out. Believing is like an empty bowl without any cracks.

486. September 17, 1993. Honolulu

When a difficult problem appears, instead of trying to solve it, the human mind would like first to run away and escape from it, as much as possible.

When you escape, at that moment you seem to be comfortable; but the problem always remains in your mind, like a dark cloud, always making you uncomfortable and causing you to be unclear.

A difficult problem is just like a bunch of threads tangled together: you do not know which to start pulling first. If solving that difficult problem is only for yourself and your own benefit, the problem will become more difficult. But if solving that problem is for others and their benefit, then that intention will find the correct thread that will enable you to disentangle all the threads; the problem will be finished.

487. September 18, 1993. Honolulu

Because of one particular person, one can be very happy.

Because of one particular person, one can be very unhappy and miserable, and suffer.

Because of one particular person, one can become a Buddha and have happiness infinitely, without extinction.

If you think of the person who causes you suffering and misery as your teacher, as one who helps you eliminate your own devil and karma, then through dealing with that difficult person you will become a great philosopher, a great psychologist and a great spiritual person. That difficult person will help you to realize what human beings are all about, and will help you to make beautiful flowers bloom on rotten logs.

488. September 19, 1993. Los Angeles

Help someone, but do not think that you are helping him.

Make a relationship, but do not think that you are making a relationship.

Teach each other to attain true happiness.

Then each of you will not receive from or give karma to one another. If you do this, you will protect each other until the relationship is finished, you will make the connection comfortable, and you will help each other to attain true happiness and have great freedom.

489. September 21, 1993. Paris

People want to be with those who make others comfortable. They appreciate the time spent with those who make them comfortable, and when they separate, they feel that they really would like to stay longer together.

This wishing to stay together makes their relationship deeper. Without feeling that they lose anything, people want to give everything to those who make them comfortable, and no matter how much they give, they feel that they did not give enough.

A humble person always makes others comfortable.

A person who has a lot of ego always makes others uncomfortable.

So remember: being humble means earning; having ego means losing.

490. September 22, 1993. Paris

If while living in suffering you realize what Buddha and Buddha's world are, you see the conditions of suffering very clearly, you can attain wisdom and realize the methods needed to come out from suffering. Then you do not see suffering as suffering; you think that such is human life, and with this human life you strive to practice and to live correctly and appreciatively.

To know Buddha and Buddha's world, one must have desperate wishes and great faith. Desperate wishes are in the place where life and death hang in balance. Great faith is in the place from which ego has disappeared.

491. September 23, 1993. Paris

Into the happy mind, the devil cannot enter.

Within the egotistical mind, there is no happiness. Because an egotistical mind is a wanting and desiring mind, it always becomes negative very easily.

When there is no desire, there is no ego. But in the happy mind which has no wanting or desire, whatever is needed always appears.

So always think about happiness and, through practice, eliminate the devil which appears from time to time in yourself.

Suffering is for happiness; happiness is in the suffering. But in the mind which has no desire, there is no happiness or suffering. That mind is full with Buddha's smile.

492. September 24, 1993. Paris

Life is always changing: good and bad, high and low. While changing, if your purpose and direction are clear, no matter how much things change, you do not have to worry about it. You just go on, whether it is good or bad, high or low.

While you go on, the changes are a good practice and experience for you, and they help make your direction and purpose much clearer. You will enjoy the changes, and at the same time, in relation to them, you will see yourself more clearly. But if you do not have a clear direction and purpose, you are just like a boat without a rudder, wandering about directionless in the big ocean, suffering.

What are human direction, purpose and goal? Let your direction become a great direction, your purpose, a great purpose, and your goal, a great goal.

What are your direction, purpose and goal?

493. September 25, 1993. Paris

All night long, I tried to make myself happy
So it was difficult to fall asleep.
In my dream, I met a spider web.
But by striving to become happy, with that mind and power,
I removed the spider web with one hand
And it disappeared, leaving behind not a single trace.
It makes me feel so free.
Until now I thought that happiness was not mine.
I thought that it was only for someone else.
But now I realize that happiness is mine too.
This happy mind eliminates all blockages and difficulties
Making me feel ridiculous that until now
I had been scared of the spider web.
Ha, ha, ha!!
Please, you be happy too.

494. September 26, 1993. Paris

Live your life without worrying.

Saying this is very easy, but it is difficult to not worry. But if you know the true path, you do not have to worry. The true path is in front of us, to the sides of us, above us and below us; it is in all directions.

When you put down one worry, you receive ten different benefits. But when you keep one worry, it creates ten different sufferings. Practice means cleaning up the path which is in all directions.

495. September 27, 1993. Paris

This is a very important teaching:
1. Give a smile, but do not give your mind.
2. Give your mind, but do not give your feeling.
3. Give your feeling, but do not think that others are yours.
4. You can think that others are yours, but do not disparage them.
5. You can disparage others, but do not think that they are lower than you.
6. You can think that others are lower than you, but think that they are your teachers who help you to see yourself.
7. You can think that others are your teachers who help you to see yourself, but respect them as your great masters who help you to become a Buddha.
8. You can respect others as your great masters who help you to become a Buddha, but do not forget the mind of deep appreciation.
9. These are eight commandments to have great relationships with others.

P. S. Why are there eight commandments? Because the number 8 (∞) symbolizes always being connected and infinity.

496. September 28, 1993. Paris

Those who make others comfortable and happy always receive love and respect from others.

Those who make others uncomfortable and unhappy are always rejected by others.

Things that make others uncomfortable and unhappy come from:
1. speech,
2. action,
3. thinking.

But if:
1. you speak nicely,
2. action becomes nice,
3. thinking becomes nice.

When you speak, act and think nicely, you make yourself important. In this way, you will be enveloped by love. In this way, you will be enveloped by respect.

Be covered with a love and respect blanket, and go to bed comfortably, every night.

497. September 29, 1993. Paris

When someone is doing better than you are, give him a compliment. When someone is not doing well, help him. Caring for others means caring for yourself. Being jealous of others is to make yourself ignorant.

Having faith in others means having faith in yourself. Others' success is your own success.

When you can work without separating yourself from others, your projects will be successful and happiness results for everybody.

The most tranquil place is the place without you or I. When you reach that complete place, then we will not need this kind of teaching.

498. September 30, 1993. Barcelona

There is infinite space around the globe. This space does not belong to one person. It belongs to everyone.

So when you have a difficult problem, do not only attach to small things and suffer. Think about the infinite space around the globe. Then your head will become clear. You will be able to take care of even difficult things without having a headache because this space belongs to everyone and is connected with everyone.

When you think about the space, there are no blockages between yourself and others; that is why you can take care of difficult things without having a headache.

When your mind is in a small space, think about large space. But when your mind is in a large space, look at things very meticulously and precisely, as if threading a small needle.

499. October 1, 1993. Ahabah

Always put the moving mind in the correct place.

If, once you put that mind in the correct place, you change the place because you become angry, jealous, or because your pride bothers you, then you become disappointed.

Always keep your mind in the place you decided upon, whether it is good or bad. Just like taking away the devil from outside, always watch yourself and do not let dust fall onto the mind which you put into the correct place; always polish it.

Putting your mind into the correct place is your self-vow, direction and promise to yourself. Become a master of your moving mind. When you become a master of your moving mind, you can see the Buddha.

500. October 2, 1993. Ahabah

While looking at the high and wide mountain in front of me,
Suddenly your face appears.
When I look at your thin and stressed countenance,
It hurts my mind.
Your smiling face, covered with fears, delusions and insecurities,
Turns my mind toward deep sadness.
I beg and ask Buddha
And I beg and ask the sky, sun, moon, mountains, oceans and land
To please help and protect you.
Having desperately begged and asked,
Seeing your face again,
I see that it is slowly opening and that energy is circulating.
Seeing your wide, open, smiling countenance makes me so happy.
Please, be happy. Your happiness is my happiness.
And do not forget that this mind which loves you
Is infinite.
Even when mountains become water and water becomes mountain,
This mind will love you infinitely and will never change.

501. October 3, 1993. Ahabah

The mind is full of happiness, but we cannot see that mind and it is easy to follow delusions. How can you see that mind?

Even though your body is in a beautiful place, if your thinking is scattered, the mind which sees the beautiful place is also scattered. Then your body, even though it is in a beautiful place, only becomes tired.

Put your thinking into one place and find the mind which can remain steady, seeing the beautiful place. Bring that mind fully into your body; then everywhere becomes paradise and with that body you can make everyone happy and help them eliminate their delusions.

In this moment, are your thinking and mind in this place?

502. October 4, 1993. Ahabah

The path of Buddha (truth, absolute, nothingness) is like daytime.

The path of sentient beings is like nighttime.

Practicing is just like finding a light in the darkness. When all delusions rest and all hindrances disappear and you become quiet and tranquil, then once in a while you can see the light. When, without dust, the light becomes strong but yet is not there, you can meet Buddha.

Buddha always gives us light; but when you are caught by your small I, even though it is daytime you do not know that it is daytime.

Practice vigorously, come out from the dark path and walk onto the bright, daytime path.

503. October 5, 1993. Paris

When the mind is looking for the mind, you can remove the dust in the mind. When the dust is removed from within the mind, then you can see the mind.

The mind that you then see is always happy. Become one with that happiness and you can enjoy true happiness. The mind which can enjoy true happiness can be a master of itself and can remove dust from others' minds and make every mind happy.

That mind which is one with others' minds eliminates mind. In the place of no-mind, everything exists with nothing.

P. S. This is a great headache teaching. The bigger the headache you get, the clearer you will become.

504. October 6, 1993. Paris

Helping others actually means helping yourself.

Helping others means making others comfortable, and not bothering or irritating them. Making others comfortable means not making them uncomfortable because of your own ignorance and conditions.

Do not affect others with your emotions and negative energy.

Helping others means, for example, that even though you are right beside someone, he or she does not notice that you are there. In order to become like this, first make yourself bright and clear and when someone asks for your help, help him or her truly and sincerely, one hundred percent. That is really helping others.

Do not draw attention to yourself, be unnoticeable, and do the job which is given to you one hundred percent. This is correct bodhisattva action.

505. October 7, 1993. Paris

Nature's energy is different according to the place. It is the same thing with the human mind: in some places the mind is positive, and in other places it is negative, sad, angry or poky.

Even though they have different karma, people who live in the same place seem to have similar personalities. This is because they are affected by nature's energy.

So once in a while, go to the place where the energy suits you in order to balance your body energy.

But if you attain Buddha's mind, wherever you are, you can realize paradise because Buddha's mind balances nature's energy and is not hindered by anything. Also, whoever has Buddha's mind is welcomed by nature, makes nature happy and is protected by nature.

506. October 8, 1993. Rhein Ruhr

When someone acts in a way that disappoints you, do not become angry; and at the same time, do not disappoint yourself.

First, check yourself to see why that person disappointed you: see your mistake. When you can clearly see your own mistake, fix it, and strive not to make the same mistake again. Also, eliminate the anger you have about being disappointed and do not hate the person who disappointed you. Hating-mind is the seed which will make you become disappointed in the future. So forget everything.

The next time you deal with the person who disappointed you, deal with him or her as if you are meeting for the very first time.

507. October 9, 1993. Rhein Ruhr

Both before you practice and while you practice, there are many things you want to do, many things you want to see, and many things you want to have. So wherever you go, you are not satisfied or comfortable. You always feel insecure and scared, and easily get excited and angry. So it is difficult to sit still.

But as your practice deepens, those kinds of things disappear one by one; wherever you go and whoever you meet, you have no fears or insecurities. Wherever you go, it is just like being in your own home; and whoever you meet, it is just like meeting someone from your own family.

Then you can see how ignorant you were, and that your fears, insecurities and suffering were all for nothing. At the same time, you can see the power of practicing and will not want to be lazy in your practice.

As your practice deepens, the whole world is just like your own bedroom and you can spend every day with a comfortable body and mind. Once in a while, delusions may appear that make you suffer. But even those you will take as an enjoyment and eliminate them one by one, in a fun and pleasurable way.

508. October 10, 1993. Rhein Ruhr

Do not expect someone else's thinking to be the same as yours. Your thinking changes all of the time, so how can you expect someone else's to be the same as yours?

If you have a person who does not bother or irritate you, but only quietly supports you, you should think that you are the happiest person in the world.

If you do not have that kind of person now, polish yourself in order not to bother or irritate others, and strive to support them sincerely and make them happy. Then in the future you will have that kind of person.

509. October 11, 1993. Rhein Ruhr

Human beings' minds are such that the more you use them in a big way, the bigger they become, just like a balloon. But if ego appears in the mind that is being used in a big way, it is just like a hole opening: the mind starts shrinking and becoming small.

Use your mind in a big way, but let go of your delusions and ego; then your mind will become bigger and bigger, like the whole universe.

In that big mind, the more you strive to eliminate your dust, the brighter and shinier it becomes, in exact relation to its size. With that shining mind you can do anything you like and you will get anything you want, because that mind is already one with the absolute mind.

510. October 12, 1993. Paris

Whose mind is it which reads these words one by one?

If you say, "My mind," you are caught by karma I.
If you say, "Not my mind," you are caught by O (emptiness).
If you say, "Buddha's mind," you are caught by Buddha.
Then whose mind is it?

In the autumn night, the sound of the falling leaves wakes me up; the gold Buddha sitting in front of me is smiling and the smell of the leftover incense stick enters my nose. Without thinking, these two hands automatically make hapchang and these lips say, "Please make all sentient beings comfortable. I will give all of my body and mind to make them comfortable and to help them become Buddhas."

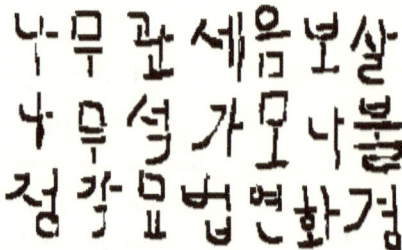

511. October 13, 1993. Paris

Truly helping others is not getting caught by their good or bad points.

Through others' good points, eliminate your own mistakes; through their bad points, check yourself once more. Strive to always make your own path bright.

When you are clear and confident, your bright actions and correct speech can truly help others. Bright action does not expect others to favor or treat you specially, and correct speech does not expect to receive any compliment.

512. October 14, 1993. Paris

Practice is to polish oneself and to not have any hindrances.

If while you practice you can see your own mistakes very clearly, that means that you are practicing correctly. But if you see your mistakes and do not see them as mistakes, insisting instead that you are right, then your 'practice' is not practice and is blocking the true path.

Right practice becomes successful when there is no thinking about 'I'. Then, even though you practice, you do not think that you are practicing; you just practice regularly, every day. You do not get caught by the practice and can polish yourself, becoming clear and bright and seeing your non-self.

Fish in the ocean drink water without thinking, but they get caught by the fish net.

Human beings on the land breathe air with thinking and get caught by themselves.

513. October 15, 1993. Munich

If you have a person to whom you can tell everything honestly, without keeping any secrets, someone who accepts you, who honestly points out your mistakes, who scolds you for making them, who guides you toward not making the same mistakes again, and who protects and makes you truly comfortable, you can say that you are the luckiest person in the world.

A true scolding is better that a sweet compliment.

514. October 16, 1993. Munich

The mind which thinks about Buddha (truth, absolute) is Buddha. The mind which has faith in Buddha is the path of eliminating one's karma. The mind which depends on Buddha is the correct method to make oneself independent and free.

That mind which has no Buddha and no I, that mind makes Buddha and makes I.

If you realize, understand and always keep this mind clean without dirtying it, this is the number one happiness in the world and leads to having the greatest wealth.

Thank you very much Buddha!

515. October 17, 1993. Munich

Always put your thinking into the bright and clear place. This bright and clear place is true I, mind, truth, absolute, love, happiness and Buddha.

While you are practicing, when you can see this bright and clear place:

you see Buddha,

you become happy,

you feel love,

you become absolute and true

you realize what mind is,

you find true I.

When you can see your true I but cannot believe in it, the reason is that you are caught by your karma, ignorance and small I.

516. October 18, 1993. Paris

Your bright and clear appearance is always in front of me.
But since I want to see you only through form,
I cannot see you.
So, what can I do?
If I see form, I cannot see you, because that form
makes me sad,
angry and disappointed.
Then, all the more I cannot see you.
But if that form is not seen as form but as Buddha,
I do not get caught by form.
Then I can see your bright and clear appearance and
I can share true, absolute love with you.
Bright and clear you,
Please forgive my ignorance, let me wake-up
Keeping clear
So that I can be with you every moment.

517. October 19, 1993. Paris

While practicing, your disliking mind, your blaming mind, your angry mind, your hateful mind, your jealous mind, your disappointed mind and your verifying mind all slowly disappear.

When any one of these kinds of mind becomes extreme—as, for example, when you hate one hundred percent—then it disappears.

During the process of all these kinds of mind disappearing, you suffer a lot. But when suffering disappears, you can see yourself very clearly, and at the same time you can see how ignorant all of these kinds of mind were. When they have all disappeared, you become comfortable and

realize that this has not been suffering but rather your great teaching.

This comfortable mind is full of happiness.

518. October 20, 1993. Paris

If you want to see Buddha (truth, absolute, true I), you must always think about and yearn for Buddha. To meet Buddha, always strive to eliminate your mistakes and blockages. Also, you must know how to love others.

If one knows how to truly love others, one already has space, knows how to understand others, and how to help them. Being like this, your space gradually becomes larger and larger, you become one with Buddha, and at that time can see Buddha. To attain this is to be adorned with beauty in this present Buddha world.

Do not see Buddha in the Buddha statue. Through the Buddha statue, which means behind the Buddha statue, see no-Buddha; then you can see the true Buddha.

519. October 21, 1993. Paris

When you do something that you like, you often get caught by what you like and your mind is not clear. That is why you can easily make mistakes. Also, even though you did what you like, afterwards, because of your unclear mind, you check and have a lot of thinking about whether what you did was right or wrong. So you waste your energy unnecessarily.

But when you do things for others and go along with what they would like to do, your mind becomes clear, you have no hindrances, and after acting you have no extra thinking. Then you become energized.

So when you want to do as you like, before you act always see yourself: is it necessary or unnecessary? If what you would like to do is in line with the correct practice path and will help you become clear and bright, then act without thinking or checking.

When you go on this path, the further you proceed, the more you become comfortable and clear.

520. October 22, 1993. Ruffieu, France

Even though you get angry, do not get caught by anger.
Even though you get jealous, do not get caught by jealousy.
Even though you like someone, do not get caught by liking.
Even though you dislike someone, do not get caught by disliking.

Then, even though the mind moves some, it will soon settle and you will not get caught even by the mind.

The person who does this is what we call a great, free person.

Shakyamuni Buddha's respectful Dharma name was Mu Ae In, which means not getting caught by anything, which is being a great, free person.

From the great, free person's mind comes great wisdom which we call unexcelled, which means utmost truth. This unexcelled wisdom makes everyone free from ignorance and leads them to the great, free world.

If you do not get caught by your complaints and judgments about others, then you can complain about and judge them. But if you get caught by your complaints and judgments, then do not even think about expressing them.

If you do not get caught by anything, you speak with a true smile.

521. October 23, 1993. Ruffieu, France

If two people have clear, bright minds, those two people become happy. But if one has a clear and bright mind and the other does not, the unclear one makes the other become unclear, too, and then they are not clear together.

When the sun is covered by a dark cloud, you cannot see its brilliance. But when the sun makes the cloud disappear, then you can see its brilliance again.

A clear person's clarity always leads the unclear person to clarity.

A clear person has no attachments, hindrances or ego, and so there is no I. That no I becomes one's master. But an unclear person has attachments, hindrances and ego, and thinks that the ego is the master.

522. October 24, 1993. Ruffieu, France

In the late autumn cold wind, make a blanket with the mantra

And wrap the mantra blanket around yourself.

Make a warm floor with the samadhi, and lie down on the warm samadhi floor.

Then make a full mind become an empty, empty mind.

In the empty mind, see the Buddha; that makes everything become tranquil.

In the empty mind, see the lover: that makes everything become loving.

In the empty mind, see the difficult person; that makes everything become compassionate.

Then, what is the thing which sees this empty mind as mind?

What is this which sees the empty mind?

What is this which feels tranquil, loving and compassionate?

And what is this which asks these questions?

What is this?

In this moment, everyone say one sentence.

523. October 25, 1993. Paris

It is very interesting to look at previous masters' realizations and enlightenment.

Some masters, with their enlightenment and realization, said "KATZ." Whatever kind of question a student asked, they said, "KATZ."

Some masters, with their enlightenment and realization, hit with their stick. Whatever kind of questions students asked, these masters would hit them with their stick.

Some masters, with their enlightenment and realization, held up one finger. Whatever kind of question a student asked, they held up one finger.

Some masters, with their enlightenment and realization, said "*Mu*" (nothing). Whatever students asked, they replied, "*Mu.*"

Some masters, with their enlightenment and realization, said, "Mountain is empty, water is empty." Whatever their students asked, they said, "Mountain is empty, water is empty."

Some masters, with their enlightenment and realization, said "Mountain is mountain, water is water." Whatever questions students asked, they said, "Mountain is mountain, water is water."

Some masters, with their enlightenment and realization, said "The mountain is green, water is flowing." Whenever students asked questions, they said, "The mountain is green, water is flowing."

However, putting all of my small I's conditions and difficulties into the wide mind space (Buddha, absolute), I use the dark cloud to make a pillow and lie down. Then the conditions and difficulties disappear, the dark cloud pillow disappears, and that I which lay down also disappears.

Mountain is mountain and is green. But in the bird's nest in the green forest, the baby bird is waiting for its mother to bring food and it cries, "Cheep, cheep, cheep!!" So the I which disappeared becomes the mother of the bird and brings food to the baby bird.

Water is water and is flowing. In the flowing water, all of the fish swim here and there, looking for food. So that I which disappeared becomes a fish and guides them all to where the food is.

524. October 26, 1993. Paris

Even if you have a worry, stop worrying and think about space.

Even if you are angry, stop being angry and think about space.

Even if you are negative, stop being negative and think about space.

When you think about space, you can put everything down. That mind which thinks about space is Buddha's mind, and that mind which believes it is Buddha's mind can connect oneself with Buddha's mind.

That body which is connected with Buddha's mind is not your own body. When you realize that, you can control your anger, worrying and negativity, and you can understand what space is. When you realize what the wide space is, you can entrust everything to the wide space.

525. October 27, 1993. Paris

Go into the tiger's cave and give food to the hungry baby tiger, but do not get bitten by his parents.

If you have this kind of wisdom, you can find yourself and you can help others.

For the person whose practice is deep, the meaning of this will be a guiding light for him.

526. October 28, 1993. Paris

The Seal of Samadhi

The seal of samadhi means eliminating your scattered mind. With this, your mind becomes very innocent and clear, and you do not even think that it is your mind. Then you become one with no-mind, go into the deep level and relax the deluded mind.

At that time, the bright level of samadhi appears and that mind doing the samadhi comes from the no-level level. That no-level level is Buddha's bright truth. Realizing this is what we call the true seal of samadhi.

When you attain the true seal of samadhi, you can eliminate the three poisons (desire, anger, ignorance) which appear moment to moment. Then you can eliminate the 84,000 delusions, you can make those 84,000 delusions into your teachers or students, and you can relax and put down the five desires (for food, fame, sex, sleep and money). Then you can use your body correctly, moment to moment, and at the same time you can protect your body and have a truthful daily life.

P. S. Someday when your practice is very deep the seal of samadhi will automatically be stamped on your head. Ha, ha, ha!!!

527. October 29, 1993. Bologna

A wise person's sentence becomes medicine for others.

An unwise person's ten sentences become a sickness for others.

When a wise person receives good advice from someone else, he or she appreciates it and uses it as a guiding light.

When unwise people receive good advice from someone else, their pride bothers them; they become angry and dislike the person who advised them.

When your ego causes you to want others to understand your situation, and you strongly want them to notice you, your ten sentences of explanation about yourself and your situation discount yourself ten times. But when you do not have expectations and do not complain to others, but only show them a calm face, that makes you tranquil and they give you credit.

528. October 30, 1993. Bologna

In the human life:
- Because of a particular person, one can become successful.
- Because of a particular person, one can fail.
- Because of a particular person, one can fail in one's deep path of practice.
- Because of a particular person, one can break the precepts.
- Because of a particular person, one can become a Buddha.

Especially in the human life:
- Because of a particular person, one can make this present world into a paradise.
- Because of particular person, one can make this present world into hell.
- Because of a particular person, one can become a hero.
- Because of a particular person, one's reputation can be ruined.
- Saving one person is just like saving 10,000 people.
- Rescuing one person is just like rescuing oneself.
- Because of a particular person, one can make bad karma.
- Because of a particular person, one can make good karma and so eliminate one's bad karma.

Keep your mind wide like space, and when you use it, use it like the hole in a sewing needle.

529. October 31, 1993. Bologna

If when you help others, you think that you are helping them and you boast to others that you did so, the merit of your helping action is lost, and because of your boasting you receive complaints rather than appreciation from others.

The action of helping others without boasting or saying anything about it is beautiful, and that action makes one shine.

Action without I always makes others happy.

Action with I (ego) always becomes a thorn which pokes others as well as oneself.

530. November 1, 1993. Paris

Today is the first of the month.

Use Buddha's mind beautifully, have beautiful intentions, think beautifully, speak beautifully and act beautifully.

Think about how to do all of this.

531. November 2, 1993. Paris

In the bright and clear sky, suddenly a cloud appears.

In the bright, clear and comfortable mind, suddenly negative thinking appears. Because of that negative thinking, one feels bad and spends the entire day in a dark cloud, wasting one's energy for nothing.

Negativity appears because of your interactions with others, and then you blame and dislike others for making you negative. You may think that you do not want to see that person again, and you easily create all kinds of delusions and projections for nothing.

At moments like this, do not lose yourself because of others. Retrieve that self which you lost because of the other person and put it back into yourself. Then the negativity which appeared because of that person will disappear, and at the same time you will be able to see your own mistake.

Seeing your own mistake eliminates the dark cloud right away, and then you can make and keep a comfortable mind. In the comfortable mind, you polish that mind again and again, and try not to make the same mistakes. You polish and polish it until the dust disappears; then you can attain true happiness.

In the non-path path,
Like wind which does not get caught by the net,
You can comfortably rest.

532. November 3, 1993. Paris

In the great love, because of cause and effect, people cannot become one with the great love; they separate from it and live in a very lonely way.

When great love sees that happen, this great love would like to help those who are lonely and it shows and gives them great compassion. But those who are deeply caught by cause and effect thinks that such compassion is their enemy and become scared.

But when you meet the dharma and practice it, you finally accept compassion's help. With compassion's help, you finally realize and truly know what great love is, become free from cause and effect, and appreciate the great love.

In that mind of appreciation, you become one with great love and with that great love never rest for even a single instant. You continuously help and do compassionate things for others.

The human body is just like candle light in front of strong wind. So while this body exists, try to do many good things and try not to do bad things. If you do this, you will not get caught by cause and effect.

533. November 4, 1993. Paris

Whatever you do, if your goal is clear and it is for the benefit of everybody, then no matter how difficult it may be to achieve, you can overcome the difficulties without having a hard time and you will succeed in achieving that goal.

But to set a clear goal is not easy. A clear goal actually comes from the bright and clear mind, and that bright and clear mind is not mine, is not yours, and is not someone else's; it is everybody's and everybody came from it.

When you set a goal in the bright and clear mind and that goal is for everybody, as you go more on the path towards achieving it, it benefits everyone and makes them happy.

So try to find your goal in the bright and clear mind.

534. November 5, 1993. Vienna

When you live quietly in the mountain with the nature where there is no one else, you yearn to have a friend with whom you can have a conversation. While yearning to have a friend, one person appears and you become so happy. But after spending a couple of days together, yours and the other person's opinions conflict with each other and you both try to show yourselves off and show how right you are.

This makes the quiet mountain very noisy, and that negative energy affects the trees and the flowers, which both shrivel, and the birds no longer sing and they lose their energy. This means that the human body and mind are connected with nature.

Even when ten thousand people live together, if their thinking, speech and action are beautiful and they use their minds in a beautiful way, then all of nature becomes beautiful and the ten thousand different things in nature grow very healthy.

When a person thinks, speaks and acts negatively, and uses the mind in a negative way, nature cannot grow around that person. Then nature's fire is just like human beings' anger; nature's earthquakes are just like human beings' nervousness and jealousy; nature's volcanoes are just like rage, jealousy and negativity which could not be held any longer and which blow up; and nature's floods are just like human beings' sadness and sorrow which gather and pour all of the sadness out at one time.

Nowadays nature's unbalanced energy is not just because of nature but is also because of human beings. In order to balance nature's energy, everyone as soon as possible should eliminate their anger, jealousy, ego and right and wrong; they should find their true selves, attain true peace, realize bright and clear mind, and in there have beautiful thinking, speech and action, and lead everyone to the path of happiness.

When everyone does this, this world will become beautiful and we will not suffer because of nature's energy.

535. November 6, 1993. Vienna

True I in Buddha's place has no ego, no good, no bad, no intelligence, no stupidity and no competitiveness; everything is calm, peaceful and round. If everyone attains this round place and realizes this roundness, then everyone will understand each other and will move and act for the benefit of one another's peace and happiness.

If everyone does this kind of action, this world would actually be Buddha's place, everyone would be Buddha, and this world would be paradise. Happiness is right in front of you and Buddha is inside of you.

When one can control one's emotions and opinions, not disparage others' opinions, and can deal with others as oneself, ego will disappear and the Buddha which is in oneself will appear and make oneself happy.

This is infinite happiness and, even though the body comes and goes, one can live in happiness infinitely.

536. November 7, 1993. Vienna

One's true I is always watching oneself. But that self always sees others and so easily becomes one with others, and therefore cannot distinguish which one is his or her own self and which belong to others'. Because of this, that one becomes confused.

When you finally meet the dharma and practice, as your practice deepens you can distinguish between your own self and others'. That self which can distinguish between the two finally comes back to you and can see the true I. In the moment you realize true I, you can see yourself and how ignorant your self has been. Then that self wants to repent for its ignorance and would like to help others. But others do not want to accept the help from that self and instead doubt about the person who is helping.

At that time, the self which knows true I repents once more, realizing that its earlier repentance in order to help others had been conditional and aimed at protecting itself. Finally you realize that when self disappears, there are no conditions and nothing to repent for. Then that self throws away even that self which takes care of that itself, and goes around just like a light cloud and a light wind. While going around, when someone calls, when someone is in need, it goes there, helps one hundred percent, and leads that person to the path of true I.

537. November 8, 1993. Paris

When you have a lot of thinking you become lazy. When you have less thinking you become diligent. Laziness makes one become a sentient being. Diligence makes one become Buddha.

Whatever work you must do today, do it today. Whatever work you must do tomorrow, leave until tomorrow.

Strive to forget what you did yesterday.

A day without thinking is a day of the bodhisattva.

A day with a lot of thinking is a day of karma I.

538. November 9, 1993. Paris

Today, recite these three sentences to yourself:

Be still.

Be comfortable.

Be happy.

Repeat each of these three times. Then repeat the mantra 108 times. Then do 108 prostrations. Then meditate for fifteen minutes.

Whatever delusion appears, for each deluded thought tell yourself, "Put it down, put it down, put it down." Imagine a big space, like the whole universe.

Then drink one large glass of water. Become one with the water, and become one with that which drinks the water. Appreciate the water and appreciate yourself drinking the water.

Then relax for 5 minutes. Your vision will become clear and you can easily find out what you must do.

Now I ask you, are you still? Are you comfortable? Are you happy?

Do not say "yes," do not say "no."

Be still, be comfortable, and be happy.

539. November 10, 1993. Paris

In the human beings' world, babies depend on their mothers' stomach for nine months and after birth they depend on their parents. While in school, children depend on their teachers and the teachings; in social life people depend upon groups and the groups' leaders; in family life the wife depends upon her husband and the husband depends upon his wife; and in the dharma one depends upon the teachings and the master.

So to survive in the human world means to depend upon others.

The person who does not like depending upon others becomes a lonely person. But the person who meets the dharma and who practices and finds the true I does not think of all the above relationships as being dependent and does not seek independence from them. Instead, that person feels sorry and regretful for having been a burden upon others and for making them worry and suffer. That regretful mind then turns into the mind of appreciation, and that person appreciates all others who take care of and support him or her, wishing to serve and help whoever is related to him or her, as well as others.

This way, one attains true independence and true freedom without being independent of and separate from others, and without being lonely.

540. November 11, 1993. Paris

Those who have difficulty living a social life go into the mountains and make friends with nature; and those who feel tired of the mountains and return to the social life are the kind of people who are not comfortable, no matter where they go. They get caught by difficulty and by fatigue. Wherever they go, it is difficult for them to adjust, and whatever they do does not last long. It is difficult for them to settle and relax, and they always invite suffering.

Practice people in the social life should take difficulties as their friends, and in the mountains they should take fatigue as their friend. Wherever they go, they should know how to enjoy their situation. They should not get caught by any place, and they should keep their brightness and clarity. Then they will know how to do their duties and perform their functions correctly.

This is the way of true practice and is the correct function of practice.

Do not be afraid of difficulty and do not boast that you can do what is easy.

541. November 12, 1993. Frankfurt

When you listen to other people's speech, you should prepare yourself so that you can listen to everything they say. Do not indulge in just liking what you want to hear and disliking what you do not want to hear. Listen to everything.

Listen again to what you did not like to hear. Then, when what you did not like to hear no longer irritates you, listen one more time to what you did like hearing. Then you will see that what you liked hearing accorded with your own opinion and that what you did not like hearing was the opinion of the other person.

Doing so, you can see that until then you had thought that only your own opinion was correct, and you will realize that you were constrained by your opinions and could not be free from them.

So whether you like or dislike someone's speech, appreciate that person who is speaking to you and appreciate the connection of conversation which you have together. Also appreciate that person for helping you to see yourself through conversing together.

Then, no matter what kind of speech you listen to, you will be able to listen to the true speech which is beyond speech. At that time, you can be free from yourself and will make tranquil whoever you are conversing with. You will help them to eliminate their belief that only their own opinion is correct, and you can have a true conversation together.

Remember, in true conversation, true love is always flowing.

542. November 13, 1993. Frankfurt

Something is nothing. Nothing is something.

If you attach to something, you fall into impermanence. If you attach to nothing, you fall into emptiness.

Do not be enchanted by the smile of the Buddha statue. See that thing which sees the Buddha statue. Then you can see the live Buddha in front of the Buddha statue.

That live Buddha transforms impermanence into permanence and transforms emptiness into existence. From time to time and from place to place, that live Buddha transforms into different bodies. It sees, helps and leads you onto the Buddha-path, and lives infinitely in the non-nirvana nirvana.

So what is this live Buddha?

"Buddha!!"

"Yes!!"

P. S. This is a very important teaching and summarizes what I have taught at the Frankfurt retreat, the last retreat of this year. Read it over and over again.

543. November 14, 1993. Frankfurt

Karma-I has a limited life span.

No-I has an unlimited life span.

When karma-I does not know no-I, it is always fearful and insecure. But when karma-I realizes no-I, it can then relax.

Karma-I always misunderstands and tries not to believe that no-I is itself. But no-I always sees karma-I and believes that someday karma-I will return to no-I. No-I always has great compassion for karma-I and always protects it with love. But karma-I does not realize the love and compassion of no-I.

But when karma-I enters the path of practice, it finally realizes what no-I is, and at that time it realizes what that love and protection is which is coming from no-I, and finally appreciates its great love and compassion.

Because karma-I would like to repay its gratitude to no-I, karma-I practices vigorously in order to become one with no-I and to be able to stay infinitely with it.

544. November 15, 1993. Paris

As your practice deepens, do not become conceited just because you think that you know many things. See that mind which makes conceit.

When you realize that in that mind there is a dust particle of conceit, you know your practice is not yet deep and that you are raising the devil of conceit.

At that time, practice to eliminate the devil of conceit and try not to be happy that your path is becoming deeper. Also, do not verify or check whether your practice is deep or shallow.

Then that path will become ripe like a fruit, and its beautiful, sweet fragrance will spread out in all four directions.

545. November 16, 1993. Paris

You can show the horse who is not thirsty where the water is, but you cannot make him drink.

Sometimes, even though a person has a lot of knowledge and skill, it is difficult for that person to relate to others. It is also sometimes difficult for others to understand and digest that person's knowledge and skill.

So try not to flaunt too much your knowledge and skill to others. Always show others according to their level and how much they can digest, and do not be disappointed if they do not follow you.

If you really want to show others your knowledge and skill, find the wisdom which is beyond knowledge and skill. That wisdom is always necessary for everyone, whether they are thirsty or not, and it gives everyone happiness because this wisdom is actually great love and great compassion.

Knowledge and skill without compassion only irritate others.

546. November 17, 1993. Paris

Because of one person, how many people can be comfortable and happy? Think about it.

If a person can make even just one other person happy and comfortable, that means that person's practice is already deep.

If a person can truly love another person who can truly and sincerely receive his or her love, then the former is the happiest person and can be happy infinitely.

One is in the many, many are in the one. When you realize one thing, you can realize ten thousand things, and this one thing will lead you to ten thousand things.

547. November 18, 1993. Paris

The dog that has doo-doo stains on his body laughs at and blames the other dog who only has dirt on his body.

People who are not clear and who do not even know how to take care of themselves only check and complain about others, try to advise them, and poke their noses into everyone else's business. Such people, even though they may practice, do not know what the path of practice is about.

For a second kind of people, it does not matter what others do; they do not care about it. Such people only do their own thing, but also think that they are always correct. It seems that these people's practice is deep, but actually they still have a lot of devils inside of them. They know what practice is, but do not yet know its true fragrance.

A third kind of person does things very well, always considers others, and considers their mistakes as his or her own. When someone makes a mistake, this kind of person feels ashamed because they know that it is their mistake, too. People like this always see their own mistakes and try not to repeat them or make new ones. They see themselves and others and practice for both themselves and others. Their path of practice is deep and they are on the way to becoming Buddhas.

548. November 19, 1993. Paris

Whenever you have important tasks, it is easy to get caught by little things and then be unable to accomplish the important things.

At that time, do not regret that there are the little things, and do not think that if they did not exist you could have done the big things better. Little things actually help you practice to do the important things better.

If you can distinguish which are the small things and which are the important things, and you go for the important things, then you can take care of both small and important matters.

So do not get caught by small things and do not be afraid of important ones. Then you can do each thing one by one, very clearly, and you can accomplish a great deal.

549. November 20, 1993. Paris

Birthday Poem

> The mind which truly congratulates the birthday is the true I.
> The mind which is happy about the birthday is the karma I.
> This karma I appreciates yin and yang,
> And at that time, yin and yang harmonize and become one.
> That oneness can see the true I which is behind yin and yang
> And so has appreciation for the true I.
> At that time,
> Karma I becomes harmonized with true I and becomes one with it.
> That oneness says:
> "Congratulations to all of you for being born into this world.
> Congratulations to all of you for existing in this world.
> Congratulations to all of you for existing together in this world.
> Congratulations to all of you for practicing together in this world.
> Congratulations to all of you for going together onto the Buddha path.

> Congratulations to all of you for your great intentions in wanting to become Buddhas
> And for trying to do bodhisattva actions.
> Congratulations to all of you for wanting to be together
> And for trying to adorn this world with beauty."
> *"Happy Birthday to You All!!!"*

550. November 21, 1993. Paris

When you know someone notices you and does very nice things for you, you would like to make that person happy and comfortable, and you would like to do nice things for him or her.

Automatically, you would like to concentrate on how best to make that person happy and comfortable. That mind which inquires into how to make others happy is not your own mind; it is actually the mind of 'togetherness'. While you are inquiring, it makes you very happy, and that happy mind makes the love you have for each other deep and truer.

Whoever can do nice things for others and make them happy has already transcended human suffering.

Those who receive love from others, even while they are in a difficult situation, did many nice things for others, and that is the reason they receive love from others now.

In the love of giving and receiving, find your true I (love I) and let the love become deeper and deeper.

551. November 22, 1993. Paris

The mirror which is polished very well is so clean that it reflects everything.

When the path gets deeper, your suffering can also get deeper because as your practice deepens you can see everything. If you do not get caught by what you see, you can eliminate the suffering. But if you get caught by it, that creates a lot of suffering.

As practice deepens, let your center become strong. Then you can eliminate all your suffering. When your strong center becomes 'no center', your truth will shine without any dust.

552. November 23, 1993. Paris

The Buddha said, "The body goes but the mind is always here."

Try to answer this kong-an: where did the body go which has gone, and where is the mind?

553. November 24, 1993. Honolulu

Wherever practice people go, even when they are in a place where the customs and other peoples' personalities are different from what they are used to, they should follow the ways of that place, but without losing themselves. And if there is anything wrong there, they should act correctly and show others the correct way.

Especially when you go to a strange place, practice harder in order to make the place of true I shine.

554. November 25, 1993. Honolulu

Seeing no-I in the empty mirror is making something-I beautiful. At that time, you can have a true taste of life. And when you make a non-stylish something-I into a stylish something-I, you can like the something-I and will appreciate life.

When from time to time you can put something-I into the empty mirror, you can understand no-I. When something-I fully understands no-I, you can live life without any dark shadows, like a bright and clear diamond, and you can live infinitely.

The trace of something-I which fully attained no-I shines more and more as time goes by and is appreciated by everyone and makes everyone happy.

P. S. This is a very important and special teaching. It is an enlightenment teaching, and if you fully understand and attain it, you will be enlightened, for sure.

555. November 26, 1993. Honolulu

When your body is healthy, your ego and pride are big, and so you do not want to be second to anyone. Then when someone hurts your pride, you become angry and think others are very bad. In this way, you make very bad karma.

But when your body gets sick and you must stay in bed, suddenly all of your pride, ego and anger disappear, and you desperately wish to be healthy again. At that time, you put your mind fully into trying to recover from being ill; you think of your doctor as a Buddha and your nurse as a bodhisattva, and you follow their directions unconditionally in an effort to become healthy again.

If a practice person still has a lot of ego, pride and anger, then that means the path of practice is still far away. But whoever follows the teachings and dharma and whoever practices without conditions will definitely go into the deep path and will succeed in attaining Buddhahood.

Those who get caught by being unconditional do not see the true I which is in the unconditional, which has transcended the conditional.

556. November 27, 1993. Honolulu

Thoughts always appear, just like clouds appearing in the bright, clear sky. But the point is, how much, and for how long do you get caught by those thoughts?

Practicing people easily put a thought into the practice mind and come out from being caught. They come back to themselves, and they can see that thought, and whether it is correct or incorrect, necessary or unnecessary. They wash away an unnecessary thought with a smile, pardon themselves for incorrect thoughts, and try not to think them again.

They put correct thoughts into action.

But if you doubt about a correct thought, that means it is not yet correct. So forget about it for the time being. When you have completely forgotten about it and have put it down, as time goes by that correct thought will make you put it into action, without thinking.

557. November 28, 1993. Honolulu

In the battle to survive, each person tries to defeat the other. If you do not want to get stuck in that battle, lower yourself one inch and fulfill your duties one hundred percent.

Then you can take care of your things very confidently without being bothered by others, and you will be respected by others. You will be victorious without having battled.

When you can give to others that victory which was won without ever having battled, you become a Buddha and a bodhisattva.

558. November 29, 1993. Honolulu

When you can think, act and speak beautifully, you can overcome all blockages and obstacles. Then no one can bother you.

No matter how heavy the rain is that falls onto the beautiful flower, it sounds soft and flows off the flower. But when heavy rain falls onto strong rocks, it makes a loud noise and makes a hole in the rocks.

Beauty always invites beauty; hardness always invites hardness.

559. November 30, 1993. Honolulu

Just because someone likes you, do not be happy about it.

Just because someone does not like you, do not blame that person.

Just because someone scares you, do not be afraid.

When you truly know where all others come from, happiness, blame and fear disappear. We come from our original, absolute place and we return there.

When you absolutely attain this, one hundred percent, you will know how to enjoy happiness as happiness; you will not blame others, and you will know how to eliminate fear. Then you can really enjoy the existence of this present life.

560. December 1, 1993. Honolulu

In love, one does not know what love is.

One gives love to others, but does not know how to love others.

One receives love from others, but does not know how to give love to others.

This means that one's walls of karma are still thick and high.

When the walls of karma become lower and thinner, you will know what love is, how to love others, how to give love to others, and how to receive love from others. And when the walls of karma disappear and you become one with love, you will know what beauty is.

In Buddha's eyes, everything is seen as being beautiful.

In sentient beings' eyes, everything is seen as being difficult and as suffering.

561. December 2, 1993. Honolulu

When you do not know the empty mirror, you do not see yourself. Then, whatever you do, it does not affect you, and if you make many mistakes, you are not conscious of them. People like this like to show off, would like to be better than others, and use their energy to be noticed by others.

But when you realize and know the empty mirror, you see yourself reflected in it. At that time, you can see how much dirt you have and how imperfect you are, and so you would like to hide yourself somewhere.

But in the empty mirror, there is no place to hide, and it only becomes clearer and brighter. You see yourself, but you cannot cover yourself with even a single thread. At that time, do not try to hide and do not be ashamed of yourself. Instead, strive to eliminate your dirt, piece by piece.

But when you eliminate one piece, another one and another one appear. So during the process of elimination, it seems that you are suffering more, and you regret that you came to realize and know the empty mirror.

But while eliminating your dirt, it is just as if white skin is beginning to appear; little by little you can see the true I, and it gradually shines more and more.

562. December 3, 1993. Honolulu

Empty mirror....
Please tell me,
For how long have you been watching me?

1 year? 100 years? 1,000 years?

You watch me all of the time,
But you do not laugh at me and you are not angry with me.
You always watch me quiescently, with benevolent eyes;
You always protect me.
Dear empty mirror,
Please forgive me for always blaming you,

And for not even once saying, "thank you."
I will strive not to besmirch you.
So I will practice every day,
Even in this moment.

563. December 4, 1993. Honolulu

In the path of human life, when you know one person, you become hindered by that one.

When you know two people you become hindered by those two.

When you know one hundred people you become hindered by those one hundred.

But even though you may know one person or one hundred people, the path to not being hindered is to always watch yourself.

Sometimes you become like a hard rock, sometimes like soft wind. But when you know that hard rocks and soft wind come and go, and that their place of existence is nothingness, then even though you become a hard rock or soft wind, you do not get caught or hindered by anything, and you can go on your life path very comfortably and freely.

564. December 5, 1993. Honolulu

Next to the devil is holiness.
Next to holiness is the devil.
Next to happiness is unhappiness.
Next to unhappiness is happiness.

The devil and holiness come from the same place, and the place of existence of happiness and unhappiness is also the same place.

When there is a bright eye, it sees the devil as the devil and holiness as holiness. At that time, the devil can remove its devil mask and become holy. Then that holiness will succeed in attaining Buddhahood, and that Buddha will give happiness to an unhappy person and will help make this happy person into a bodhisattva. That Buddha will then help lead this bodhisattva to be able to help everyone, to share the happiness, and will also lead him to becoming a Buddha so that he or she can have infinite happiness.

565. December 6, 1993. Honolulu

When someone else makes a mistake, realize that it is your mistake.

When someone else is happy, realize that this is your happiness.

Before you complain about another person's mistake, see your own mistake first. If you truly want to help others, do not point out others' mistakes with poky speech; make them realize their mistake through your soft action.

A wise person's speech is like a beautiful fragrance. An unwise person's speech is like a needle into others' hearts.

In the round moon, soft wind makes the moon brighter, and that bright moon shines everywhere.

566. December 7, 1993. Honolulu

Practice the path.

In the path, live with Buddha brightly and clearly.

When you come out from there and return to the sentient beings' world, however, you become confused and you do not know what to do because you forget. At that moment, while you are in this kind of situation, think of the Buddha and do the mantra. Then, no matter what kind of confusing situation you are in, you can easily connect with the Buddha. This makes you bright again, and you will know what to do without getting caught by any situation. You can go on your path of practice and can realize and appreciate the power of the practice path.

567. December 8, 1993. Seoul

The karma home town is a very interesting place.

You left the karma home town a long time ago, and when you returned, it was familiar. But after knowing what the true I's home town is, it makes the karma home town uncomfortable and uneasy.

Meeting your karma family is a happy encounter, but you are not comfortable with one another because somehow something is blocked; you cannot really have a trusting and comfortable conversation. At that time, you realize how important the dharma family is, and you really deeply appreciate the dharma family which you have.

I wish for all karma families to become truthful dharma families so that everyone can be happy and comfortable with one another. I wish for this day to come as soon as possible.

568. December 9, 1993. Seoul

People's footsteps move very quickly. But if you know where the footsteps are going, you can stop them once in a while and think about the true I for a moment.

If you think about the true I, even while taking a busy step you can connect with and be protected by the true I; then busy footsteps can proceed in a relaxed way. Your path will always go in a correct way so that you can truly enjoy the human path.

This is just like going onto the "freeway" of life rather than onto the "highway" of life.

569. December 10, 1993. Seoul

When you are wandering in your thoughts and come out from there and can see yourself, you then realize that you had many thoughts. You also realize that thoughts are just like dreams, and that when you're caught up in them, you miss the present moment; you wander in these dreams, and even though you are awake and it is daytime, it is like you are deep in the night.

While you are in those thoughts, that thing which knows they are thoughts is your true I. That true I is always buried in the thoughts; it is just like a diamond buried in the dirt.

Practice is like removing the dirt, discovering the diamond, and making it shine. At that time, even if the thoughts come and go, you do not get caught by them. Instead, you become the master of your thoughts: if you want to have thoughts, you have them; if you want to put the thoughts down, you put them down.

Like this, you can always have an interesting life.

570. December 11, 1993. Seoul

An unwise person complains about others.

A wise person knows how to give compliments to others.

When you complain about others, that complaint comes to you.

When you give a compliment to others, that compliment comes to you.

Those who know how to give compliments to others are those who have space for themselves. That space will lead them to a deeper path and will make them a hero.

Compliments make beautiful fragrances, and those fragrances make everyone happy.

571. December 12, 1993. Seoul

When you want to be successful and realize whatever wishes arise, do not wait for someone to help you, and do not complain and be disappointed just because someone is not helping you. First, concentrate and put your mind into helping others, and always inquire into how to make others happy.

When you act this way, unexpected happiness and success will come right in front of you. This will make all of your wishes come true and will make you happy.

Your happiness and success are actually everyone's happiness and success. One penetrates 10,000; 10,000 penetrate one.

572. December 13, 1993. Honolulu

When there is a situation which can make you disappointed and angry, before you become disappointed and angry, give yourself space for a moment and feel that space with wisdom.

The method to feel a space with wisdom is to not get caught by disappointment and anger, and to think about how you can take care of that situation wisely. That thinking will give you space, that thinking will make you wise, and that thinking will handle the situation wisely.

Buddha is always in front of your eyes. But human beings' minds always look far away, and that is why they always invite suffering.

573. December 14, 1993. Honolulu

Bury the 84,000 delusions in silence.

Bury all conditions and discrimination in silence.

Bury your sycophantic and self-beneficial speech in silence.

In silence, find Buddha and have a true conversation without speech. Then, if you open your mouth, whatever speech comes out will never irritate others, will never hurt others, and will always be appreciated by the person who is listening to you.

Even if you think your speech is correct, before you speak out, put your thinking into silence for a moment, at least one time. Then what you say will be valuable and, even though you do not force it, it will shine and be beautiful.

574. December 15, 1993. Honolulu

Most sicknesses come from the mind. When the mind is comfortable, even if there is a sickness it heals. When the mind is not comfortable, all kinds of sicknesses appear.

The mind is the master of the body, and the body is the master of using the mind. So how you use your mind determines whether you are healthy or not. When you use your mind in a humble and good way, you become healthy. When you use your mind in an arrogant, angry and jealous way, you become sick.

If you realize that the place of the mind is Buddha and that you are Buddha, then you will realize that the causes of all sicknesses derive from yourself. In order to eliminate these causes, practice every day and make yourself comfortable. Have a comfortable mind. That will make you healthy, and then your one word which comes from your comfortable mind will be medicine for someone else's sickness.

575. December 16, 1993. Honolulu

No matter what kind of situations we are in, let us strive to live today beautifully.

No matter what kind of situations we are in, let us strive to live today just like Buddha.

No matter what kind of situations we are in, let us strive to live today just like a bodhisattva.

When you strive to live in these ways, all of your karma and blockages disappear, and all the luck and happiness will follow you. Then you will have lots of prosperity and happiness in this life and in life after life.

576. December 17, 1993. Honolulu

When there are many things you must do, you may not know how to handle them. At that time, think about Buddha (absolute). Then, automatically you will know how to handle doing all of those things; your confusion will disappear; you will accomplish the doing of each thing, one by one; and even though you do many things, you will not get tired and you will appreciate your job.

Thinking of Buddha (absolute) is Buddha's thinking, and that Buddha's thinking is what makes you become a Buddha. That self which makes you become a Buddha, and that Buddha, will always know how to rescue themselves, no matter how difficult the situation.

577. December 18, 1993. Honolulu

In a suffering situation, one does not know what beauty is.

In a beautiful situation, one does not know what suffering is. But if one realizes that we are presently in the beautiful (absolute) world, one is not hindered by either a suffering or a beautiful situation. Rather, one will know the cause of suffering and the cause of beauty, and according with each situation and others, one will know how to eliminate suffering and keep beauty.

You are then not hindered by either suffering or beauty, and are not into either of them for yourself. If someone else is suffering, you suffer; if someone else is happy, you are happy.

With that mind, one keeps beauty eternally.

578. December 19, 1993. Honolulu

To make a difficult decision about something and to decide to put your strong attachment down is not easy. Also, when you put your strong attachment down, you feel as if you lost something and you feel very empty.

Yet, if you really put your attachment down one hundred percent, completely unexpected benefits will come in the near future. When you put your attachment down, however, do not think for even a moment that unexpected benefits will come.

Truly putting your attachment down means: without thinking, cutting the water with a knife.

579. December 20, 1993. Honolulu

Today is a day during which you must work diligently. Eliminate lazy mind, strive to be diligent, eliminate confused mind, and continue on your direction and path.

According to the situation, you can become either lazy or diligent. The human mind is such that you can easily become lazy. But when you are diligent, you can keep the way of diligence. So always keep yourself in the clear way so you can have a beautiful life in Buddha's beautiful world.

The meaning of taking a holiday is not being lazy. Taking a holiday means relaxing with a clear mind and preparing yourself to continue going on the correct direction. So relax, but be clear.

During a holiday, clearly see yourself in the glass of champagne.

580. December 21, 1993. Honolulu

As your path gets deeper, your eyes become clearer and you can see others better. For example, you can see what kind of energy they have; you can see if someone is negative or positive.

But even though you see, if you meet someone who is negative, it makes the situation and yourself negative too. When you know that, practice much harder so that you do not get caught by someone else's negativity: try not to be either too close with or too distant from those who are negative, and do your duty.

581. December 22, 1993. Honolulu

In Buddha's world there is no anger, suffering or sorrow; it is only bright and clear. But sentient beings' world is not like that; there, many things are always appearing, and it is difficult to be comfortable.

Those whose practice path is deeper have wisdom and power, and are able to travel between Buddha's world and sentient beings' world many times in one day. They know how to enjoy Buddha's world and how to enjoy sentient beings' world. But because they do not want to get caught by either of those worlds, they always polish themselves so that their no-I will always shine.

582. December 23, 1993. Honolulu

What is the most important thing in the world? It is the practice life.

What is the greatest happiness in the world? It is attaining enlightenment.

What is the most difficult thing in the world? It is living a long life without getting sick.

Practicing and attaining enlightenment are just like having the most precious jewel in the world. With that jewel, you can do whatever you want and you do not have to be subject to ego, anger, jealousy, agony or worry.

But our body is different. Because it is borrowed from nature, someday you have to give it back to nature. So while we have this body, appreciate it; have a comfortable mind and do many good things for others. Then you can live a long life without having too much sickness.

But if, because of your karma from the last life, you get sick and do not live a long life, if your mind is comfortable and you do good things for others, then you are paying back what you owe to nature. Then, next life, you can have less sickness and live longer.

583. December 24, 1993. Honolulu

Look at all forms which appear in this world in a compassionate way.

Look at all living being forms in this world in a compassionate way.

Look at all living forms struggling to survive in this busy world in a compassionate way.

When you look at forms in these ways, the mind that can love everything automatically appears, regardless of whether that thing is good or bad for you, or whether it benefits you or not.

584. December 25, 1993. Honolulu

Two thousand five hundred years ago, Shakyamuni Buddha appeared in order to save all sentient beings.

Nineteen hundred and ninety-four years ago today, Jesus Christ appeared in order to save all sentient beings.

Their great intentions, love and compassion have been passed on to sentient beings until today. It is because they connected their attainment and truth with sentient beings that their teachings have been passed down and are still circulating today.

But because unclear sentient beings' eyes have been caught by good and bad and right and wrong, until today sentient beings discriminate and think, "Buddha's teaching is good," or "Christ's teaching is good," or "Buddha's teaching is wrong," or "Christ's teaching is wrong." Through their discriminatory thinking, sentient beings dirty and deeply confuse themselves.

Practice people, do not discriminate and do not judge; only appreciate Buddha and Jesus Christ's great intentions. So when you see the Buddha, appreciate the Buddha; and when you see Jesus Christ, appreciate Jesus Christ. Yet, practice vigorously to make yourself bright and clear so that you do not get caught by either of them. Only have a great intention to become Buddha yourself, as soon as possible, and go on the path to save all sentient beings.

Let your footsteps, one after another, only go in this direction. December 25, 1993. Merry Christmas!

585. December 26, 1993. Honolulu

We can say that human's life span is short or we can say that it is long. But if we clearly realize that our life is like a lit candle in front of the wind, then, while we have this form, we will not want to act ignorantly; and by not acting ignorantly we can automatically eliminate the three poisons.

But when we do not realize this and we think that we are the only ones who are going to live long, it is difficult to eliminate the three poisons.

When we are twenty, thirty or forty years old, this sentence seems to be somebody else's business. But when we become fifty, sixty or seventy years old, then we can easily hear it as our own business.

586. December 27, 1993. Honolulu

The Buddha said, "Losing money means that you have lost many things, and losing a friend means that you have lost even more. But losing faith and belief means that you have lost everything."

The mind of faith and belief in Buddha and the absolute, the mind of faith and belief in the mantra (energy line), and the mind of faith and belief in the teachings is the mind which leads you to find yourself.

Finding yourself means rescuing yourself from karma and blockages. So if you do not have faith and belief, and if you do not practice, you cannot find or see your own Buddha.

587. December 28, 1993. Honolulu

When the situation appears in which you seem able to get everything you always wanted, if at that time you do not get everything you always wanted, you are still completely satisfied. Also, at that time you can check whether or not what you wanted is really necessary, if it is for yourself or for others. Being able to check that makes you even more satisfied.

The reward of having the situation of being able to get what you want comes to you because of your faith, belief and practice. Having faith, belief and the practice is just like having a magic diamond and with this diamond you can do whatever you want.

Let us practice regularly in order to get this magic diamond so we can have complete satisfaction, life after life.

588. December 29, 1993. Yun Hwa Dharma Sah

As a wise people's paths deepen and they come to know better what Buddha is, they feel ashamed and become humble. Such people appreciate their teachers who make them realize what Buddha is, and they appreciate the practice.

Even if the path of those who are unwise deepens and they know a little of what Buddha is, they confuse themselves and believe that they are already Buddha. People like this become very arrogant and say that their teacher is not their teacher. They do not appreciate their teacher and think that they are already enlightened and know everything.

The quiescent Buddha sees everything very clearly and brightly, and with pity sees the sentient beings appearing and disappearing. That Buddha always wants to lead them onto the Buddha-path and help them to eliminate their suffering. Also, while sentient beings exist, that Buddha shows them how not to make bad karma and leads them onto the correct path so they can become true Buddhas themselves.

589. December 30, 1993. Yun Hwa Dharma Sah

Buddha's realm is a bright, clear, beautiful and comfortable place.

With a sentient being's mind, it is difficult to imagine the realm of Buddha and is difficult to even believe that it exists. With a sentient being's mind, it is also difficult to think about true clarity, brightness and beauty.

But as one's path deepens, one realizes that there is the realm of Buddha, and even though it may not be too clear at first, one begins to realize the existence of true clarity, brightness and beauty.

As one slowly realizes this, it is possible while in the realm of sentient beings to conquer and eliminate one's difficulties oneself. Also, in order to come out from the realm of sentient beings, one realizes that one desperately needs to have patience and endurance.

Then, one effortlessly knows how to endure everything, and that endurance actually automatically leads one to the realm of Buddha; that mind of endurance makes one a Buddha. This Buddha travels freely between the realm of sentient beings and the realm of Buddha, and into whichever realm he travels, he or she makes it shine, brightly and beautifully.

590. December 31, 1993. Yun Hwa Dharma Sah

When you can see the bright and clear realm of Buddha, your karma disappears; and after this, when you make karma, you only make bright and clear karma. Bright and clear karma is bodhisattva karma. Then, all of your actions, thinking and speech rescue others, make them happy, and at the same time lead them to the bright and clear realm of Buddha.

If you want to see the bright and clear realm of Buddha, first you should look at everything positively; second, you should always think optimistically; and third, you should neither regret the past nor have expectations about the future.

Everyday only wish to see the bright and clear realm of Buddha and practice for that. Then even though you do not want or expect anything, either while in the realm of Buddha or while in the realm of sentient beings, everything appears and you accomplish in the emptiness whatever you must. You can really do your true job, infinitely.

www.ingramcontent.com/pod-product-compliance
Lightning Source LLC
Chambersburg PA
CBHW022006160426
43197CB00007B/303